THE JESUS TRADITION

Gerard S. Sloyan

the Jesus Tradition

IMAGES OF JESUS IN THE WEST

Foreword by Donald Senior, C.P.

TWENTY-THIRD PUBLICATIONS
Mystic, Connecticut

For Mary Perkins Ryan
and Carolyn Nicosia

ISBN 0-89622-285-3
Library of Congress Catalog Card Number 85-52138

Cover design by George Herrick
Interior design by John G. van Bemmel

Foreword

This book keeps good company. As its author readily acknowledges, it joins a long line of thoughtful works by Christians of every age and every viewpoint who have tried to capture in words the mystery of Jesus Christ. Gerard Sloyan is not an amateur in this struggle; his long list of published credits has several titles on christology, including his book, *Is Christ the End of the Law?*

What makes this a different effort than many of the others is that he peers over the shoulders of other theologians and mystics (sometimes the roles are joined) to chart how they have attempted this difficult craft. His book is a study of images of Jesus forged in Western Christianity from the fifth century until the present time. As he points out, the christological controversies of the first few centuries of the church led eventually, with much pain and heat, to creedal formulations. The creeds helped set the framework within which the church could reflect on the mystery of Christ but the bare assertions of the creeds, however sound and necessary, could be no substitute for the rich brew of symbol and story and ecstasy found in the biblical witness to Christ. In the church's piety, in the contemplative insights of its mystics and in the writings of its theologians the spare frame of the creed has taken more meaty and palpable shape.

This book traces some of those images of Jesus with competence and with sympathy for both the value and limits that each particular historical and cultural milieu imposes on every image of Jesus, no matter how sacred or serviceable. No Christian exists in solitary fashion. Jesus was not the savior of a series of individuals, Fr. Sloyan reminds us, but of a community of people. We need our history, just as much as we need the biblical revelation. And so, as the author humbly states, we need not just one or two but twenty-two, or more, perspective books like this.

Scanning the titles of the more than score of books he has written, one can appreciate how Gerard Sloyan's own rich history has led him here. The bulging shelf of his publications is dominated by works on christology, liturgy, catechetics, preaching, Scripture, and ecumenism, particularly in the area of the Christian-Jewish Dialogue. Beneath those titles are consistent interests that dominate the tone of his writing, including this book. He shows a profound interest in the Scriptures, especially the gospels. He has a continuing interest in the prayer and worship of the church, not only as the vital source of the church's spirit but as a catalyst for its thought. He is committed to informed and sensitive communication of the Christian message. This latter interest which prompted his pioneering works on religious education has, in more recent years, developed into a consistent ecumenical thrust to his writings. Those who know Gerard Sloyan personally are aware that the breadth and largesse of such academic interests reflect not just intellectual pursuits but his own personal spirit.

It is a genuine honor to write a foreword for a book such as this. Not only as a tribute to a fine Christian scholar who has contributed so much to the life of the church in this country, but also because it is a timely book. As the following pages demonstrate, the church's image of Jesus has been shaped by its historical experience. As is obvious to everyone, we live in a world and a time when swirling historical forces have put us in a situation of significant change. What may be less obvious is that the milestones of historical change — crossed by almost every generation — have for our times been further enriched, or complicated, by worldwide cultural exchange. As Karl Rahner reminded the church, we are on the brink of a new age when perhaps for the first time in its history the Christian church is becoming a "world church," that is, a church not only with members in various parts of the world, but a church whose theology and worship is being shaped by the experiences of Christians from many cultures and subcultures—a phenomenon our Western-dominated church has not experienced for a long time.

This book focuses on "Images of Jesus in the West" but its author is fully aware that there is more than the West to deal with in shaping our understanding of Christ. However, before we can be adequately prepared to be enriched by the insights and instincts of Christians of other cultures we would be wise to be more thoroughly in touch with our own history. There are some moments in our past, such as the writings of the English mystics, that only now are being appreciated. That is one of the important values of a book like this in times like these.

If, in fact, our church struggles to be truly universal and open to the faith expressions of manifold cultures, the church—and the world — will be the better for it. The Jesus of the New Testament was a man who lived in a complex cultural milieu, a Middle Eastern society steeped in Jewish faith, profoundly influenced by Greek culture and under the political control of Rome. The thrust of Jesus' ministry, and of the community formed in his name, was to cross boundaries. As Fr. Sloyan has demonstrated in this and other books, precisely within that interaction of the transcendent with the human — a human enfleshed in Jewish and Greco-Roman culture — the New Testament itself was born and the first images of Jesus were shaped by a community of faith. Under the impulse of the Spirit, with much struggle and no little triumph, that process has continued throughout the centuries of the church's existence until the present day. This book illustrates some of the results of this vital reflection. And, by bringing a wider audience of Christians into contact with their heritage, it serves as an invitation for this process of life-giving reflection to continue.

Donald Senior, C.P.
Catholic Theological Union
January 10, 1986

Contents

Introduction

Every age gets the Jesus it wants and needs. No age gets the Jesus it deserves. This figure of mystery, however he is viewed, is pure gratuity: God self-given for those who believe in him as the Word incarnate, a human being writ larger than our puny race for those who do not.

Was Jesus a person whose mental states and emotional responses we can reconstruct from what we know of him? Or is he a historical cipher we fill in with our own conceptions, whether of the perfect human or of limitless perfection, deity itself?

Novelists and dramatists have attempted the reconstruction of Jesus ever since those art forms were first developed — drama by way of liturgy — in a Christian milieu. The reconstructions fall woefully short. What story, play, or poem comes to mind which includes Jesus as a character and develops him like the rest, which then is acclaimed great art? None, surely. Perhaps it is the wisdom of the centuries that accounts for this, the most gifted in the literary craft abstaining consistently from this foolhardy venture. Is it the skill of the evangelists that has succeeded in putting them off? The figure of Jesus in all his simplicity found in their portrayals may explain the later reticence.

The iconographers are not hesitant here, nor the painters and mosaicists. Why should that be? From the painters, it is true, you often get an Armenian or Greek, a Fleming or Italian of youthful intensity whom you might encounter on any street or byway. You do not get the Son of man. That is why the representations in two dimensions — apsidal Christs, illumined icons — are more successful than those in three. The striving for human realism defeats the purpose, "for, behold, something greater than Solomon is here... something greater than Jonah is here." The attempt to convey some touch of deity by word or brushstroke often conveys how little the person of art has wrestled with the mystery of godhead in humanity.

✳ The nameless monks and nuns of ages past seem to be an exception to this rule. In their restraint of pigment or tile they show much by what they do not show. If you have risked your life for "God from God, Light from Light, true God from true God" — and many did in those violent times of dogmatic struggle — your brush is moved to convey some hint of the creedal reality.

People do in fact express themselves and their epoch by their images of Jesus. They always have and always will. Every hope and dream, even disappointment and frustration, finds its way into the parabolic speech that goes to make up paeans of praise to the Lord Christ or a reported revelation or an exhortation to piety. Jesus as people present him is alternatively male and female, overwrought and controlled, intellectual and emotional. He is often androgyne, a coincidence of opposites. He is now Coptic, now Celtic, now Indian or Chinese. To be sure, the claim is always made that there is no departure from Matthew, Mark, Luke, and John or from Paul and his disciples or the other epistolarians or apocalyptists, of whom John of Patmos is the chief. These provide the canon of the Jesus image, fleshed out as the Christ of Isaian and Pauline and Johannine faith by the great creeds and councils.

But it was not long before the gnostics and other heretics of the second century found the scriptural portraits of Jesus too tame for them. The early generations had thought him to be both Word of God and mortal man. This latter carnal view needed correction, some thought. The heavenly Christ had to be portrayed as the product of eternal Mind, coming forth twinned in the first of pairs from deity's Fullness. In gnostic hands Jesus fled our human company.

Was he not, others asked, all verbal shading left aside, our God who shed his blood for us? Did not the Father beget in him the multiplier of miracles from infancy onward? Already in the time after the apostolic age the elaborations had begun, not in one direction but three, five, myriad directions.

⚹ The Great Church held the line against all these myths and fables by dint of a clear-cut device. It fixed a canon, saying that the authentic Jesus of divine and human reality could be found in these 27 books. Any embroidering of the image or sharp departure from it was neither the Jesus of history nor the Christ of faith. Believers were at the time incapable of that neat distinction, of course. There was only a Jesus Christ of history's faith. When creeds were hammered out to cope with the ingenuity of dreamers and intellectuals who found the Jesus Christ of the New Testament too unsubtle or too crass, the Jesus Christ of the creeds was required to be the one of the canon of Scripture.

Such creedal selection was severe. ⚹

The phrases chosen for the creeds left aside far more than they included. All the sayings of Jesus by which we know his ideals and his outlook are gone. So are the human touches the evangelists occasionally allow themselves. There is left in the heart of the Apostles' Creed simply a Jesus Christ who is divine: "His only Son, our Lord"; and who is human: "Conceived by the Holy Ghost, born of the virgin Mary," condemned to die by a civil servant remembered for his cruelty, buried in the pit of "hell" (because truly dead) and then encountered alive: "On the third day he rose again." Ascended to God's right hand, "thence shall he come to judge the living and the dead." Such was this Son of God, this man among men. In a later elaboration he is "begotten, not made, of one subsistence with the Father; through him all things were made."

In this way the image of the Jesus Christ whom the New Testament presents was made firm: truly divine and truly human. The pious excesses of St. Ignatius of Antioch are curbed by the process and not only those of the ones who came after him, disdainful of the careful plodding of the Scriptures. A Christ of creedal commitment, however, has taken over from the living, breathing Jesus of the gospels. Even when these portray him as a wonderworker and a seer, and they often do, the gospels begin to be read with the eye of Nicaea, Constantinople, Ephesus, and Chalcedon.

Jesus had always been an object of faith, even if before his resurrection it was faith of a tentative sort. After the christological councils he is seen largely with that conciliar faith. The struggle had been long and hard. Christians everywhere were part of it. But even when the one-nature people were shown to be less than Catholic in the divine-human amalgam they arrived at, the image died hard. A landless proletariat is not stirred by the thought of another victim sufferer like itself. A God in human dress who is unrestrained by human limits is boundlessly attractive. Declared heretical, the conception nonetheless has a life of its own. Put to death in the church's great assemblies, it refuses to remain interred. And so we have the Jesus Christ of "popular monophysism," the great and orthodox Cyril's unwitting legacy to the church. From the fifth century on and forever after there will be the struggle to uncover the Jesus Christ of the apostolic deliverance in the Christian Scriptures: truly inexpressible divinity, truly one of our race; a single individual in whom there is no confusion or commingling of the divine and the human.

Paradox is not the right word for this faith of the church. Rather, mystery beyond the power of human intellect to plumb. Paradox *is* the right word for the verbal games the church fathers liked to play in conveying both divinity and humanity complete in this one Jesus Christ. St. Augustine of Hippo was the master of paradox in the West, and for a thousand years he reigned in his masterful portrayals of the humility of Jesus which raised us to lofty eminence. The technique is called in rhetoric *auxēsis* or amplification. By it, "the augmented instances rise to a height of great beauty and grandeur." Thus:

> He was wearied with earthly journeying who has made himself the way to heaven for us; he became as it were one dumb and deaf in the presence of his revilers, through whom the dumb spoke and the deaf heard; he was bound who has freed human beings from the bonds of their infirmities; he was scourged who drove out from human bodies the scourge of every pain; he was crucified who put an end to our torments; he died who raised the dead to life. But he also rose again, nevermore to die, that none might learn from him so to despise death as though destined never to live hereafter.[1]

This Latin-speaking master of human psychology led a chorus of those who recovered Jesus the Galilean from the gospels, Jesus who lived and loved and taught and died, seeing in him also Christ the universal redeemer. Here is St. Leo the Great, less lyrical than Augustine but no less intense:

> He took upon himself all our weaknesses which derive from sin, he who had nought in common with sin, that he might lack nothing of hunger or thirst, weariness or sleep, grief or tears in his affections, and that he might endure the most wrenching pains even to the extreme of death.[2]

Throughout the centuries this Jesus, a figure of compassion, was viewed as savior of the human race from its condition of mortality and sinfulness. He was an intercessor with God, a divine person of strength and power, a lover of humanity, a fellow sufferer with multitudes on life's journey.

As the ages unfolded, every conceivable change was rung on these basic images of Jesus. The variety was wide. It differed from culture to culture and people to people, yet always Jesus was viewed as Lord of the church and head of the body

which the church is. Nothing in the New Testament sustains the
view that the reign of God comes to individuals rather than to
a community. This is a modern idea. Jesus nowhere abandoned
the Bible's basic relation of God–People of God. He was not
perceived to have done so until the highly individualistic age of
the Renaissance. Until then he was seen as thoroughly correla-
tive with that reality of the future, the church as the full gathering of Israel and the nations. As the glorified Christ, Jesus is
what the church is called to be. The Christian as an isolated
monad in relation to the isolated and heavenly Christ is an idea
that could not have occurred to a desert solitary. Up until the
sundering of Christian unity in the West he dwelt in a heavenly
company of angels and saints and was in living, corporate communion with all believers on the earth. There was a constant
interaction between the faithful "on the way" and the Lord Jesus
to whose abode they were journeying. They made the journey
as a body of believers, not as single ones. The few who were
saints among them gave indication to the rest of what the Christ
of the cross and resurrection was like. One needs to study the
lives of the saints for a true account of the many ways in which
Jesus was imaged in East and West. They who had arrived in
glory had caught something in the human frame of the immense
holiness of God. What Jesus summed up in his person they pos-
sessed in fragmented fashion. Their lives are the best narrative
of the varieties of Jesus-imaging in many times and places.

In his recent *Jesus in Focus* (1983) the present writer tried
to show how the evangelists and Paul were the pioneers in interpreting Jesus to their communities. A weakness of that book
is its reliance on the homogeneous aspects of the first three
gospels. In fact, Mark and Matthew and Luke each selected
his traditional materials in such a way as to give a quite distinct
interpretation of the significance of Jesus. The intent is clearer
in John's presentation but the uniqueness of each of the other
three is indisputable.

The chapters that follow pursue the same search as that
first book in a variety of postbiblical writings. What is the

rationale for the selections that have been made here? A trail was followed, after the period of the christological councils, which certain great spiritual teachers of the West had blazed. Every writer selected in this book represents, and in some cases is responsible for, a new way of imaging Jesus in the lives of millions. The chief problem in such a venture is that many portraits of Jesus are necessarily left aside. Where are the great German and lowland mystics? it may be asked. Where is the treasury of Russian spirituality? Tauler and Ruysbroeck are not here. Neither is St. Theodosius or St. Sergius or St. Nilus Sorsky. The Irish contribution is a simple absentee.

> The thorns of his head, the spike in his footsoles,
> the spear in his pap, the nail in his palms—
> may these wound me, O God
> tho' it be not enough to pay for thy blood.
> May I bear the cross beside thee, may I drink the
>   drink of gall;
> tho' to drink it were dire poison to me,
> may I sit with thee at one banquet.

Not everyone will concur that the choices made are the wisest. Defending one's options is surely time lost. One can, however, regret the option of avoiding any direct discussion of the periods in history that gave rise to the images of Jesus. Jaroslav Pelikan in his *Jesus through the Centuries: His Place in the History of Culture* (1985) entitles his concluding chapters, The Universal Man, The Mirror of the Eternal, The Prince of Peace, The Teacher of Common Sense, The Poet of the Spirit, The Liberator, and The Man Who Belongs to the World. There is much more sociology and cultural history in that admirable book than this. At the very least, that is why two books are better than one and twenty-two better still. "There are still many other things that Jesus did, yet if they were written about in detail, I doubt there would be room enough in the whole world to hold the books to record them" (John 21:25). An editor once said that. He thought that an excellent interpretation of Jesus that he had come upon, in what are now the first twenty chapters of John, could be bettered. And so he set himself to do it.

The work of seeking a fresh image of Jesus in the life of a believing people has never ceased.

The "Apostolic Fathers"

Saint Matthew concluded his gospel by having Jesus say to his disciples whom he had assembled on a high mountain in Galilee: "And, behold, I am with you all days until the end of the eon" (Matt. 28:20*b*). That is a fairly wooden translation of the Greek, but it attempts to convey Matthew's statement about the persistent presence of Jesus with those who would believe in him. It has been a foundation stone of church life ever since. This gospel-writer was the protagonist of the idea of a "called-out assembly" (*ekklesia*) which we speak of in verbal shorthand as the "church" (Matt. 16:18; 18:17). Matthew, toward the beginning of his gospel, featured a cryptic story from the book of Isaiah (7:14) to convey his conviction that in Jesus God is with us (Matt. 1:23). Both at the beginning and end of the Matthean gospel God is with us in the person of Jesus Christ. There is no church without a Christ and no Christ without a church.

Jesus, the Galilean Jew of the troubled first century of our era, has been a living presence to believers in him over all the ages since. He will be such, Christians believe, until the present *eon* — a term in Greek translation that Jewish apocalyptic thought used to divide historically the dealings of God with Israel — comes to an end. Jesus is with the church in memory, but not only so. He is present in mystical union as head of his body the church (a figure found in the epistles to the Colossians and the Ephesians). He is no longer simply the itinerant prophet, "mighty in word and work," who died as a criminal. He exists as one raised up by God from the dead to live the life of the new eon — "exalted in glory at the Father's right hand," as a combination of phrases from the Christian Scriptures says of him. This glorification by God has made him Lord and Christ, Savior and Redeemer. Israel's LORD has already appointed him a "Messiah for you," says an early Peter speech (Acts 3:20), "whom heaven must receive until the time of universal restoration which God spoke of long ago by the mouth of his holy prophets" (v. 21).

We have, then, the reality of a Christ in glory with the Father "there" and a Lord of the church which is "here." To both of these, some prefer the Jesus of the brief, pre-exalted earthly days described by the evangelists as the one with whom to be in continued contact through prayer. This is fine so long as believers realize that Jesus was already an object of religious faith by the time the gospels were written. The evangelists never provided us with portraits of a mere Jesus of history. He is already a Christ of faith in the least theologically developed gospel, Mark.

Historical Jesus and Heavenly Christ

This Christ who is believed in was a historical person, to be sure. Some of the church's earliest censures were directed at those who believed in him as the heavenly Christ only, wishing no part of the historical Jesus. Both his humanity and his

Jewishness made certain second-century gnostics ("knowers")
skeptical and impatient. This was a "carnal" Jesus, they main-
tained. The sole interest of these earnest intellectuals was in
a "spiritual" Christ.

Saint Irenaeus, bishop of Lyons (d. circa 202), was an early
opponent of this wrongheaded spiritualizing tendency. Yet just
as wrong is the tendency in our day — the ancient world would
have been mystified by it, even some in the Jewish world who
did not see in Jesus the agent of God appointed to be revealed
as Messiah — to hail Jesus as a great teacher but not one in
whom "the fullness of deity dwells bodily" (Col. 2:9). A Jesus
Christ bereft of either his humanity or his divinity is a Christian anomaly, a person devoid of reality.

Understandings of Jesus
in the Christian Scriptures

In a book published in 1983 entitled *Jesus in Focus: A Life in
Its Setting* (Mystic, Conn.: Twenty-Third Publications), I tried
to convey something of the faith portraits of Jesus painted by
the four evangelists between the years 70 and 100, and the faith
convictions of Paul found in his extant letters which date to
circa 50-56 (as well as those of his disciples which date to ca.
60-100). Complementary to this treatment is the careful
exploration of the numerous formulas of faith in Jesus Christ
scattered through the Christian Scriptures in *This Man Jesus:
An Essay Toward New Testament Christology* by Bruce
Vawter.[1] Professor Vawter looks into the great expressions of
the earliest proclamation, among them 1 Cor. 15:3-8; Phil.
2:6-11; 1 Pet. 2:22-25; 3:18-22; Acts 3:13-26; Rom. 1:3-4; and
texts in the wisdom tradition like 1 Cor. 1:21-24 and John
1:1-16. It is an admirable handbook of a variety of christologies
of the Christian Scriptures, namely, the way various believers
and communities of believers viewed Jesus in the seven decades
after his resurrection.

Expositions of the Jesus Christ of most of the various books of the Christian Scriptures are fairly common. Unfortunately, treatments of the christologies of Hebrews and Revelation and James, not to mention the apocalyptic 2 Peter and Jude, are not so easily come by. People tend to think that they have descriptions of the earthly Jesus in the gospels and of the theology of redemption in Paul, and that the two together are quite sufficient for them. These tidy distinctions are not quite true, of course. There are four different christologies of Jesus in the four gospels — which are not biographies but only seem to be. There is another christology in Paul's letters and still others in Ephesians and the pastorals (1 and 2 Timothy, Titus). The remaining epistles and treatises (including Hebrews, which is not, as many believe it is, an epistle) are all ways of proclaiming that the Jesus of history is the Lord of the church and the Christ of its faith. The twenty-seven books of the canonical collection are thus more alike than unlike. Each has as its main concern a particular christology, that is to say, a way of viewing Jesus theologically.

Biblical and Nonbiblical Writing

We hope to be examining in the pages that follow the ways various Christians of the centuries viewed the Jesus in whom they believed. This should be both an interesting and important study. The creeds like the Apostles' and the Nicene and the christological councils of Ephesus and Chalcedon, which were superimposed, so to say, on the Christian Scriptures, have reduced to a certain few the readings of Jesus our Lord allowable within Christian orthodoxy. But the actual possibilities realized in the past were much richer.

We will begin our inquiry with the writers of the second century. Conservative evangelical Christians tend to grow impatient with any such study as the one we plan. They think that the Bible contains everything anyone needs to know about Jesus Christ and salvation. If they examine the writings of the century after the apostolic age (roughly A.D. 30-125, hence 125-225), they are shocked that these writers did not simply quote from the books on Jesus that are found in the Christian Scriptures. But the earliest nonbiblical authors not only had not yet identified any Christian writings as Scripture, but they were widely thought to have written inspired Scripture themselves. It was not until 200 or so that the lists of books thought to be dependable as writings of the apostolic age (the "Canon") began to come clear. Even then, some writings that ultimately *did* make the list of those normative for faith were not accepted in certain churches (e.g., 2 Peter, Revelation), while others that did *not* survive as part of the canon were accepted (e.g., the *Didachē*, 1 Clement). To complicate matters further, the church fathers up to the medieval period distinguished between *inspired Scripture*, which included most of the extant second-century writings, and *canonical Scripture*, the twenty-seven books that came to be agreed on as part of the Bible. The lists that contained the exact twenty-seven books we have today began with one compiled by Saint Athanasius in 367.

The "Apostolic Fathers"

Who were these "apostolic fathers," as the writers of the second century came to be called, and how did they view Jesus Christ? The term for them was devised in 1672 by a French scholar named Jean Cotelier, on the theory that certain early writings had the simplicity and freshness of the apostolic writings in the canon. He published two volumes which contained the letter ascribed to Barnabas ("Pseudo-Barnabas"), *The Shepherd* by Hermas, two letters of Clement of Rome (the second of which later turned out to be an anonymous homily), seven letters of Ignatius of Antioch and one of Polycarp of Smyrna, together with an account *(Acta)* of the latter's martyrdom. Another writer named Andreas Gallandi a century later added the apologetic letter addressed to Diognetus and the fragments of Papias of Hierapolis and Quadratus. In 1873 a collection of

ethical teachings was discovered joined to a handbook on how
to celebrate baptism and the Eucharist and how to deal with
wandering prophets, *The Teaching* [Didachē] *of the Twelve
Apostles.*

These are the early writings of which we are speaking.
All are in Greek, all are orthodox (i.e., none contains much
that was later accounted heresy, or is gnostic, that is, in search
of a higher spiritual knowledge that despises the material as
unworthy of having a part in salvation); and they encompass
almost everything Christian we have from the second century.
Some additional works in this grouping are the Apologies of
Aristides, Justin, Tatian, and Athenagoras; also the Odes of
Solomon, and the Coptic collection of Jesus' sayings known
as the Gospel of Thomas, defended by some as partaking in
a wisdom christology which is not gnostic. Irenaeus's *Five
Books Against Gnosis Falsely So-Called* comes at the end of
the century.

Turning to the first non-canonical writing of the second
century (parts perhaps from ca. 70, other parts from ca. 125),
we find Jesus represented in the *Didachē* by some sayings and
the Lord's Prayer in their Matthew form. Jesus is spoken of,
in the eucharistic prayer to God, as "your child" (or "servant" — the word is *pais*). Glory and power are God's "through
Jesus Christ forever." In the prayer-phrase, "Let Grace come,"
"Grace" is probably a word for Christ at the last day. He is
also "the Lord," in whose name traveling teachers must be
received as if they were he himself. This Lord has a "Lord's
Day" on which his "pure . . . sacrifice" must be offered in the
breaking of bread and giving of thanks. Jesus is a mediatorial
figure in the *Didachē*, but also one who will come at the end
"with all his saints . . . on the clouds of the sky."

In 1 Clement (ca. 95-100) the author inveighs against envy
and rivalry in the Corinthian church, calling on what seem
to be extra-canonical collections of sayings of the Lord in
chapters 13 and 46. Thus, Jesus is quoted as saying, "Show
mercy, that you may be shown mercy. Forgive, that you may

be forgiven. . . . As you give, so will you get. . . . As you show kindness, so you will receive kindness." There is also the beginning of an extra-biblical theology of redemption in 1 Clement: "Let us reverence the Lord Jesus Christ whose blood was given for us."[2] He is "our salvation . . . the high priest of our offerings, the protector and helper of our weakness. Through him we fix our gaze on the heights of heaven. In him we see mirrored God's true and transcendent face. . . . Through him the Master [God] has willed that we should taste immortal knowledge."[3] Jesus Christ is "your Child,"[4] the author says to God, "the high priest and guardian of our souls,"[5] "our defender,"[6] the one whose "magnificent and holy name has been invoked" on believers.

If these references to Jesus seem liturgical and somewhat distant psychologically, the later correspondence of Ignatius of Antioch written on his way to martyrdom (ca. 110) is marked by intimacy and warmth. There is at the same time overt reference to Jesus' divinity such as we do not find in the Christian Scriptures. As Savior he shed "God's blood."[7] He is "that life from which we cannot be torn,"[8] the "one physician . . . born yet unbegotten, God incarnate, genuine life in the midst of death . . . first subject to suffering then beyond it";[9] one who will be "within us as our God."[10] There are unbelievers who say "his suffering was a sham,"[11] but these "are none of the Father's planting."[12] Jesus Christ is he who "became the perfect man."[13] The Eucharist is "the flesh of our Savior, Jesus Christ, which some deny."[14] Where he is, "there is the Catholic Church."[15] This "Christ God"[16] is "above time, the Timeless, the Unseen, the One who became visible for our sakes, who was beyond touch and passion, yet who for our sakes became subject to suffering, and endured everything for us."[17] (Polycarp 3,2). These epistles, written from shipboard by Ignatius on his way to martyrdom, represent a very high christology, yet the mediatorial office of the human Jesus is never forgotten. The following seems to be taken from an early creed:

> Be deaf, then, to any talk that ignores Jesus Christ, of
> David's lineage, of Mary; who was really born, ate, and
> drank; was really persecuted under Pontius Pilate; was
> really crucified and died, in the sight of heaven and earth
> and the underworld. He was really raised from the dead,
> for his Father raised him, just as his Father will raise us
> who believe in him, through Christ Jesus, apart from
> whom we have no genuine life.[18]

One finds in both Clement and Ignatius passages that betray
an awareness of Saint Paul's teaching on justification by grace
through faith rather than by human effort. This theme does
not, however, predominate. It is one among many others. The
power of Christ's blood to save is perhaps the leading theme.
There is no interest shown in any of the second-century
material in the details of Jesus' public life, either in the four
gospels or non-canonical sources. We shall see in a subsequent
chapter the mad scramble of the third and fourth centuries to
reconstruct Jesus' career by supplying details not found in the
canonical gospels.

The attractive, legendary *Martyrdom of Polycarp* contains the following creedal fragment:

> We can never forsake Christ, who suffered for the salva-
> tion of the whole world of those who are saved, the fault-
> less for the sinners, nor can we ever worship any other.
> For we worship this One as a Son of God, but we love
> the martyrs as disciples and imitators of the Lord, deserv-
> edly so, because of their unsurpassable devotion to their
> own King and Teacher.[19]

In another place Jesus Christ is called "the Savior of our souls
and Helmsman of our bodies and Shepherd of the Catholic
Church throughout the world" (19,2). Polycarp's life of fidelity
culminating in martyrdom is praised as one lived "according
to the gospel of Jesus Christ."[20]

The long and convoluted treatise of Hermas (apparently a wealthy Roman), *The Shepherd*, deals with sin and repentance in a series of five visions, twelve mandates, and ten similitudes. It contains little about Jesus Christ, having mostly to do with God as "the LORD" of the Septuagint Greek Bible, with occasional references to the Holy Spirit as someone grieved by sin. When Jesus is spoken of, it is as the Son of God.[21] Under the figure of a great tree, the Son is God's law "given to all the world . . . preached to the ends of the earth."[22] The LORD, "being long-suffering, wishes those who were called in his Son to be saved."[23] In other images, the Son of God is "rock," "door," and "gate... the only entrance to the LORD."[24]

The Letter to Diognetus is philosophically inclined and develops the idea of Jesus as the beloved Child to whom alone was communicated God's "great and unutterable design" for the world. "When he revealed it through his beloved Child and made known the things that had been prepared from the beginning, he granted us all things at once."[25] In one lyrical outburst the anonymous author writes: "The sinfulness of many is hidden in the Righteous One, while the righteousness of the One justifies the many who are sinners. [God] showed the Savior's power to save even the powerless, with the intention that we should have faith in his goodness, and look on him as Nurse, Father, Teacher, Counselor, Healer, Mind, Light, Honor, Glory, Might, Life — and that we should not be anxious about clothing or food."[26]

This last quotation indicates the struggle of the writers of the second century to combine phrases from the gospels newly in circulation with Greek philosophical concepts. At times they bring us up short with an expression of faith that has not survived into the modern world. In the main, however, they show a surprising "modernity" of doctrinal phrasing, especially from the time of Justin Martyr's *I Apology* (ca. 155) onward. None of these writers has the modern curiosity to know about the deeds of the earthly Jesus, his mental state, or psychological responses. The second-century writers are satisfied that Jesus' indisputable humanity, in all its weakness, is wedded to the power of the eternal Son of God. Their concerns are unrelievedly doctrinal. A passage from Justin may serve to summarize the writings of the period on Jesus:

> The Word himself has shown that you will not succeed, and after God who begot him we know of no ruler more royal or more just than he. . . . He foretold that all these things would happen — our Teacher, I mean, who is the Son and Apostle of God the Father and Master of all, that is, Jesus Christ, from whom we have received the name of Christians. . . . We have learned that he is the Son of the true God himself, and hold him to be in the second place and the prophetic Spirit in the third rank. It is for this that they [i.e., pagans and Jews] charge us with madness, saying that we give the second place after the unchanging and ever-existing God and begetter of all things to a crucified man, not knowing the mystery involved in this, to which we ask you to give your attention as we expound it. [27]

This report is perhaps incomplete without citations from Saint Irenaeus's *Five Books Against Gnosis*, commonly given the descriptive title, *Against Heresies* (ca. 180). They would not, however, enlarge the picture of Jesus already given. Three are given below (p. 34) which stand for many more. He is human in every respect, his chief office is mediatorial as between God and sinful humanity, and he possesses as Son of God uniquely divine power.

On the Way to Nicaea

The second century portrait of Jesus is such that we are not at all surprised to see him spoken of creedally in the fourth century as "true God and true man." As in Saint Paul's epistles, a binitarian scheme (Father and Son) is encountered far more often than a trinitarian. When the Spirit is spoken of it is sometimes personally, sometimes not, so that the late settlement of the ambiguity about the Holy Spirit as the equal in subsistence of Father and Son (defined at I Constantinople, 380-81) is readily understandable.

Phrases like that of Justin Martyr quoted above speaking of Jesus as "in the second place" after God represent the search for a working vocabulary on the mystery of godhead only beginning to be reflected on. There is enough reference to Jesus Christ as deriving from the Father in his deity and being a creature in his humanity that the mid-third-century "subordinationist" teaching of Novatian in Rome is entirely comprehensible. So, too, is the teaching of Arius of Alexandria (ca. 320) that Christ is "the first-born of all creatures" through whom all else was made. In his zeal to protect the uniqueness of godhead, Arius taught that the one "begotten by God" (namely, the Son) equalled the one "created by God." The judgment of the church at Nicaea was against him. But he could teach what he did as a deacon in good standing by dismissing the clear attribution of divinity to Jesus in the letters of Ignatius, for example, as an unsophisticated failure to preserve the indivisibility of godhead. At the same time he pressed hard the Christian Scriptures and the second-century texts that speak of that which is derived and created in Jesus Christ.

Anyone who looks for a development of Jesus' human character in the second-century writers will be disappointed. Such is not their interest. They are very concerned to deny that he merely *seemed* to be human without being such in fact ("docetism"). But this emerged as doctrinal affirmation, not as an exploration of what he was like as a human being. We shall have to wait for the not always doctrinally sound "apocryphal gospels" for that.[28]

Early
Apocryphal Images
of Jesus

The portraits of Jesus that we
have in the gospels were probably put in their present form
in the seventh and eighth decades of the first century. None
of the evangelists sat down and said: "Now I will write a canonical book." Each one wished to fix in writing the message of
Jesus Christ as it was known to him from the tradition. All four
testified to the revelation of God in Christ by assembling the
sayings of Jesus, the miracle stories, and the exorcistic accounts
they were familiar with and weaving them into a coherent narrative that resembled a biography. In none of the four cases
was the resulting gospel a true "life of Jesus"; rather each formed
a statement of belief in what God had done through Christ — a
statement that *looked* like a biography of Jesus.

Earlier still, Saint Paul in his correspondence utilized a
written form other than the narrative one. In the 50s, from

which all his extant letters come, there were not yet any written gospels in Greek, only oral and written fragments of preaching that would later be incorporated into the gospels. Did Paul know them or know about them? Analysis of his epistles shows that he had a remarkable grasp of the "words of the Lord," but he never cites them biographically. Perhaps he did not know what would emerge as the Palestinian gospel tradition. Or it may be that he knew it but did not wish to give the impression that one had to have known Jesus in the flesh to be his authentic apostle. In any case, what we have by the year 100 or 125 is a body of writings being read in Greek-speaking assemblies all around the Mediterranean that gave testimony to who Jesus Christ was in the design of God. Some were couched in the form of biography (the gospels); most were not, being letters or catechetical instructions (for adult baptismal candidates) or quasi-theological treatises (like Hebrews) attempting to persuade hearers about the truth of the "message."

Within the next century, writings with Jesus at the center proliferated, so that by the year 200 or so Christians were deciding which of their scriptures should be called dependable, setting the standard (or "canon") of apostolic faith. This process included a decision not only on Matthew, Mark, Luke, and John but also on the numerous gospels that were intended to take the place of the four or to provide an enlargement that would stand side by side with those reckoned genuinely apostolic.

In these apocryphal gospels (the word *apocryphal* means "hidden" but came to mean "spurious"), the writers worked up stories and legends about Jesus in the form of novels aimed at supplementing information thought to be deficient. Often these filled in the silence found in the gospels about Jesus' parents or his home life in the early years. In such cases the writings were a genuine response to curiosity. Often they were written from a standpoint that later came to be judged heretical. Examples are the heightening of Jesus' divine power at the expense of reporting his human limitations or making him utter statements about himself that the gospel writers thought were doctrinally true. These gospels were largely products of the second century. In the next century there was a spate of apocryphal "Acts," telling where the various apostles traveled and how they preached the gospel. These often turned out to be the gospel the authors favored rather than that of the apostolic age.

A list of canonical books (again, those dependable for right faith) was found in 1740 in Milan by a scholar named Muratori. The listing came from Rome and was written some time before the year 200 in faulty Latin by a native speaker of Greek. It is largely our familiar Christian Scriptures with a few additional books — some spoken of favorably, a few warned against as "forged for the sect of Marcion." This Muratorian canon does not list any apocryphal gospels. A catalogue from the sixth-century Decretum Gelasianum of southern Gaul, by contrast, does. It mentions gospels under the names of the apostles Matthias, Barnabas, James the Less, Peter, Thomas ("used by the Manicheans"), Bartholomew, and Andrew, plus others attributed to Lucian and Hesychius. An important source on these early books — many of them destroyed by the church in the name of orthodoxy or lost — is the writings of the fathers and others who are not accorded that title. Thus, from Saint Justin Martyr, Origen, Tertullian, Clement of Alexandria, and Eusebius of Caesarea, we get isolated sayings of Jesus that were not included in the canonical gospels. Many are sublime and well worthy of the Lord. So, for example, "Ask for the great things and God will add to you what is small," is attributed to Jesus by Clement. Origen quotes the better known: "The one who is near me is near the fire; the one who is far from me is far from the kingdom."

Gospel of Thomas

A collection of 114 sayings of Jesus, known as the Gospel of Thomas, was discovered at Nag Hammadi in upper (i.e., southern) Egypt in 1945. The saying about the fire quoted by

Origen appears as number 82 in this collection. For the first few decades after the collection came to light it was thought to have been composed of canonical sayings that had been re-arranged and added to in a Gnostic spirit. More recent scholars are convinced that numerous canonical sayings of Jesus which it contains preceded in form the form they acquired in the four gospels. Some even think that the Gnosticism attributed to other Thomas sayings is overblown because of the tenor of the library holdings among which they were found. These students of Nag Hammadi hold that an orthodox wisdom chris-tology, which later became Gnostic, sufficiently accounts for the wording of the sayings. An example of such a disputed *logion* (or "saying") follows:

> Jesus has said: "If those who lead you say to you: See, the kingdom is in heaven, then the birds will fly into heaven in front of you. If they say to you: It is in the sea, then the fish will go before you. But the kingdom is within you and without you: If you know yourselves, then you will be known, and you will know that you are offspring of the Father, who is the Living One. If, how-ever, you will not know yourselves, then will you fall into poverty. And you are poverty."[1]

The Thomas collection, while called a "gospel," is not truly one because it has no narrative component. Various early Christian writers report to us the existence of three actual non-canonical gospels, which they knew firsthand. These are *The Gospel of the Nazareans, The Gospel of the Ebionites,* and *The Gospel of the Hebrews.* Saint Jerome says that the first was in use among Syrian Jewish Christians and was closely related to canonical Matthew. The document of the *Ebionites* (meaning "the poor") was in Greek; it was likewise closest to Matthew, and departed from what came to be doctrinal orthodoxy in certain important matters. Clement and Origen are the two chief witnesses to *The Gospel of the Hebrews,* which also seems to be heretical and not especially related to any canonical gospel.

How do the fragments of these three gospels cited by early writers contribute to our knowledge of the way Jesus was viewed in the second and third centuries? The answer is: hardly at all. We learn from *The Gospel of the Nazareans* that when the mother and brothers of Jesus invited him to be baptized by John (cf. Matt. 12:46; Mark 1:4; Luke 3:3) he said: "In what have I sinned that I should go and be baptized by him? Unless what I have said is [a sin of] ignorance." This conveys a defensive mentality — the same as that found in Matt. 3:14 — at the thought that Jesus might have received the penitential sign out of need. In addition, *The Gospel of the Nazareans* contains elaboration at Matt. 18:21f. about forgiving up to seventy times seven times: "For even in the prophets after they were anointed with the Holy Spirit, a word of sin was found." The man with the withered hand (cf. Matt. 12:9ff.) is a mason who had earned his livelihood with his hands and who asks Jesus to restore him so that he may not have to beg his bread in shame. Apropos of Jesus' word about households that are divided over him (Matt. 10:34-39), a text in Eusebius's *Theophany* quotes *The Gospel of the Nazareans* as saying: "I choose for myself the most worthy; the most worthy are those whom my Father in heaven has given me."

Epiphanius of Salamis (fourth century) is the chief citer of material from *The Gospel of the Ebionites*, all of which, with two exceptions, expands verses of the canonical gospels. The exceptions are these: Jesus is described in this gospel as "created as one of the archangels" and as responding to the question "Where do you wish us to prepare the passover for you?" with "Do I desire with desire at this Passover to eat flesh with you?"

In contrast to the other two non-canonical gospels and the synoptics, the cited passages of *The Gospel of the Hebrews* tend to have Jesus speak in Johannine style. They also include a few bizarre conceptions. A mighty power, Michael, came into the world as Mary "and Christ was in her womb seven months." "The Savior says, 'Even so did my mother, the Holy

Spirit, take me by one of my hairs and carry me away onto the great mountain Tabor.' " At the Lord's baptism, "the whole fount of the Holy Spirit descended upon him and rested upon him and said to him: My Son, in all the prophets I was waiting for you that you might come and I might rest in you. For you are my rest; you are my first-begotten Son who reigns forever." And from Jesus' lips the more comforting: "And never will you be joyful except when you behold your brother with love." Cognate with this is the reckoning among the most onerous offenders in *The Gospel of the Hebrews*, "He who has grieved the spirit of his brother." These two sayings resemble Thomas 25: "Jesus said: 'Love your brother as your self, guard him as the apple of your eye.' "

Still More Apocrypha

A dependable source for all this extra-canonical material is a work compiled by E. Hennecke–W. Schneemelcher, translated by R. M. Wilson, and entitled *New Testament Apocrypha*.[2] It appeared in Germany in that edition in 1959 and comments on about fifty *logia* of the *Gospel of Thomas*, as well as on many extant fragments and whole books. Needless to say, all 114 sayings in the Thomas collection should be consulted. These appear in another English translation in James M. Robinson (general ed.), *The Nag Hammadi Library*,[3] a book that provides numerous Gnostic expositions of the significance of Jesus Christ from that Coptic monastic library discovered in 1945. Among these are *The Gospel of Truth, The Apocryphon of John*, and *The Gospel of Philip*. They all contain some familiar gospel data but are much more concerned with eon speculation centering on the heavenly Logos. Jesus' coming in the flesh is recorded in these tracts but then explained so spiritually that the reader has to doubt the authors' deep commitment to the incarnation as the Catholic tradition understood it. The various translators and editors in Robinson's volume provide introductions, but the material in the documents requires that the reader possess a good knowledge of Gnostic thought for much comprehension to take place. If the object is gaining an expanded picture of Jesus, little is lost by ignorance of the Gnostic world. As noted above, the chief concern of the authors is with the pre-existent Logos and the heavenly Christ.

Clement of Alexandria quotes a *Gospel of the Egyptians* in his *Stromateis* ("Miscellanies," lit., "Tapestries"), defending marriage and the begetting of children. In the treatise a certain Salome converses with the Lord, who tells her that death will have power " 'as long as you women bear children' — not as if life were something bad and creation evil [Clement explains] but as teaching the sequence of nature." Clement quotes *The Gospel of the Ebionites*, attributing this sentiment to the Savior: " 'I have come to undo the works of the female' [Clement goes on], the female meaning lust and the works birth and decay." The Alexandrian does not oppose the idea that female passions are powerful. He grants it, saying that this is balanced by the predominant male passion of wrath. His polemic is against the Egyptians' contention that Jesus delivered us from sexual intercourse. *The Gospel of the Ebionites* contains a saying of Jesus given in different wording in 2 Clement and Thomas 22: "For the Lord himself, on being asked by someone when the kingdom should come, said: 'When the two shall be one and that which is without as that which is within, and the male with the female neither male nor female.' " No stand is taken here against sexuality or even for androgyny; rather, the resolution of all opposites in a higher harmony at the Last Day is favored. This is usually dismissed as a Gnostic sentiment. It could be that. It could also be a saying of Jesus reflecting the Jewish apocalyptic outlook that none of the evangelists incorporated.

Gospel of Peter

A fragment of a *Gospel of Peter* was discovered in Akhmim, upper Egypt, in 1867. It does not seem to present more than the canonical gospel material, but it works out numerous details in a reasoned, apologetic way. The gospel has one unusual feature. On the cross, between two malefactors, Jesus "held his peace, as if he felt no pain." He called out from the cross: "'My power, O power, you have forsaken me!' And having said this he was taken up." While soldiers in watches kept guard over the tomb before "the Lord's day dawned" (a sign of both late composition and lack of sophistication), "there rang out a loud voice in heaven, and they saw the heavens opened and two men came down from there and drew near the sepulcher." The stone rolled aside of itself, the two men entered the tomb, and three emerged, "two of them sustaining the other and a cross following them, and the heads of the two reaching to heaven, but that of him whom they led by the hand higher than the heavens. And they heard a voice out of the heavens crying, 'You have preached to those who sleep,' and from the cross there was heard the answer, 'Yes.'"

A fifth-century Coptic gospel, which bears a Greek title meaning *The Wisdom of Jesus Christ*, has been known since 1896. A still older manuscript copy (fourth century) was found at Nag Hammadi in 1945. The gospel is Gnostic in spirit and contains one unique detail about the Redeemer *(sōtēr)*; after giving the disciples the greeting of peace in Johannine form (20:19; 14:27b), he "smiled and spoke to them: 'What are you thinking about, or why are you at a loss, or what are you seeking?'" The present writer knows of no other mention in early Christian literature of Jesus' smiling. The essence of the Greek gospel *Sophia Iēsou Christou* — for it is not much interested in the earthly Jesus — is contained in its account of the risen Savior who summoned the twelve disciples and the seven women who had followed him as disciples to a mountain in Galilee, where, "appearing to them not in his original form but in the invisible spirit . . . [he had] the appearance of a great angel of light." He instructed them about "the true nature of the universe, the plan of salvation, providence, the excellence of the powers, and all that the Redeemer did with them . . ."

The Book of James

The roots of *The Book of James* (in the sixteenth century dubbed the *Protoevangelium*) go back to about 150. It was written to establish Mary's miraculous birth and perpetual virginity. This it does through supplying the details of her parents' domestic life, betraying at the same time a painful ignorance of Jewish customs. Joachim, a very rich man, is married to the childless Anna. He is turned back from offering his gifts to the LORD because of his childlessness. Anna, meanwhile, puts on her bridal garments and seats herself under a laurel tree to bemoan her condition, saying that, "even the birds of the sky are fruitful before you, O LORD." An angel announces that she will conceive, and Joachim, in his joy, offers calves and kids from his flock.

The child — Mary — comes in due course, walking precociously at six months and entertaining an assembly of high priests, priests, and scribes at her first birthday party. She is taken to the temple at the age of three, placed on the third step of the altar, and left there to be nurtured like a dove and to receive food from the hand of an angel. When she turns twelve the priests have a problem about her "polluting the temple of the LORD," presumably by menstruating. Then follows the well-known, miraculous rod story. Widowers are assembled, each with a staff, and from Joseph's a dove comes forth to fly onto his head. (In another gospel his rod flowers.) Joseph is old, the father of grown sons, and he fears becoming a laughingstock with this young girl (Mary), so he leaves her in his house while he goes off to "build my buildings." By the device of casting lots, Mary is assigned to weave garments for the priests. She is also scolded roundly when Joseph discovers her to be six months pregnant. He knew he should not have absented himself — as Adam did at the hour of prayer, when a visiting serpent stopped by. And so on. Jesus comes to birth in a cave attended by Joseph's sons, while Joseph goes "off to Judea" to give place to the three wise men.

James continues to tell his story in support of Mary's virginal status. Little credit is given to the restraint of the holy pair. The story features, rather, Joseph's age and the total unlikelihood of his fathering the child. It ends in surprising bloodshed with the murder of Zechariah in the temple. Herod's soldiers, in search of the infant John, capture and make an end to the father. Jesus, meanwhile, is safe because Mary hears of the search, is afraid, and "wrapped him in swaddling clothes and laid him in a manger." The tale is surprisingly like a modern historical novel: pulp fiction produced for a pious purpose. More recently its television equivalent has been called "docu-drama."

Another infancy story — written in Syriac and Greek under the name of Thomas the Israelite — primarily depicts Jesus as an infant prodigy. Irenaeus (d. ca. 202) knew about it. In this gospel Jesus at twelve cleanses the ford of a brook with a word, makes twelve (real!) sparrows from soft clay on the sabbath, and gives the son of a scribe a withering glance, in the strict sense, for dispersing the water of a stream Jesus had gathered. "You insolent, godless blockhead," Jesus says winsomely, "What harm did the pools and the water do you? See, now you shall wither like a tree and shall bear neither leaves nor root nor fruit." The exasperation quotient of the young Jesus runs high, but this mayhem is in the interest of having the townsfolk exclaim, "What child is this?" or words to that effect.

Jesus, in this gospel, finds his teacher deficient in knowledge, catching him on the meaning of the letter *A*, and instructs him allegorically so that he can move on to *B*. On the good side, Jesus resuscitates a dead boy and heals the split foot of another lad who had endured the stroke of an axe. The setting becomes clear when Jesus says at the end of the tale (a Thomas-like *logion*): "Arise now, cleave the wood and remember me."

In a later Arabic infancy gospel a girl who is suffering from leprosy is cleansed of her illness by the bath water of the little Jesus. "There is no doubt," the townsfolk say, "that

Joseph and Mary and this child are gods, not men." Date palms bow down and yield their fruit to Mary in Egypt at the command of her infant son. The miraculous is present in abundance in these tales; but equally so is the unorthodox use of catchwords from the Christian Scriptures (cf. Acts 14:11). Jesus calms the dragons who come out of caves, acts as a shepherd to little children who have turned into goats, and in general proves his divine power by extravagant deeds. The gospel miracle narratives are sober by comparison. The human Jesus of Nazareth is almost nowhere to be seen in the dizzying profusion of apocryphal gospels.

An exception of a slightly different order may be the five books of *Memoirs* compiled by Hegesippus about 180 to combat the myths of the Gnostics. Eusebius's *Church History* (A.D. 325) is our source on Hegesippus, whose work we no longer possess.[4] That earlier Semitic Christian has some material on James the Just, brother of the Lord, which parallels the account of Josephus; thus, when he describes the influence of the family of Jesus in the early church he should not be dismissed out of hand. The menfolk probably did act as a kind of caliphate, as he indicates; but a detail such as the account of Saint Joseph's brother Clopas who fathered Simeon, the second "bishop of Jerusalem" after James, is at the very least anachronistic in terminology and probably untrustworthy. The same must be said of stories of Joseph's first wife Salome featured in other gospel fragments, not to speak of solutions to the problem of the Marys of the canonical gospels. Complete genealogies are not lacking — all of them doubtful in their entireties.

The natural curiosity of believers that stoked the fires of these fanciful tales is understandable. So is the novelistic aspect of the stories in a culture that circulated romances every bit as furiously as does ours — for oral repetition, of course, not private reading. We might wish that the literature in sum provided us with some new information about our Lord, but it does not. What we have is a reworking of biblical motifs from

both testaments, to which have been added details of out-
rageous fancy. Descriptions of Jesus' personal appearance, for
example, show him ruddy-faced and handsome like David — or
repulsive to look upon because the Isaian Servant Songs say
there was no beauty or comeliness in him. There is no plumbing
of his motivations such as is found in a later literature. His
human status is taken for granted; but since it is not the stuff
of great entertainment and his divine power *is*, we get these
writings. A mixture of reasons — apologetic, doctrinal, and
"reader-gratifying" — combine to feature the marvelous above
everything else in apocryphal literature.

A reading of this apocryphal literature is strongly recom-
mended in order to heighten appreciation of the compositions
of the four canonical evangelists.

3

From the
Church Fathers
to the Early Middle Ages

In the last two chapters we searched out images of Jesus from sources dating after the Christian Scriptures (and perhaps before) — first in the sayings collection known as the Gospel of Thomas and various second-century writings, then in the apocryphal gospels of the third century and following. If the canonical gospels portrayed him theandrically — fully human and fully divine, without notable imbalance — the fictitious biographies of a later time did little more than clumsily grind their doctrinal axes, while apologetic and doctrinal treatises worked hard to refine theologically the church's faith in him. Both were done without especially advancing our insight into the kind of *person* he was, as we would say today. The tendencies that later became "orthodox" and "heterodox" were too busy exploring his divine personhood in human manifestation, a dogmatic concept.

Perhaps the search for reflection on the personality of Jesus, nontheologically understood, in those early centuries is futile. The churches of the East and West came to rely on the four canonical gospels as dependable apostolic memoirs of Jesus, and they preached them in the churches. The patristic age did not treat him novelistically as the authors of the apocryphal romances did. Neither did they probe his motivations, human responses, or psychological states as they might have done. They simply found humanity and deity inextricably united in him, viewing him increasingly from a Johannine perspective as the revealer of the Father come from heaven in the flesh.

God Using the Word in Our Humanity
to Save us

Saint Irenaeus of Lyons is a fairly early entrant on the formal theological scene. His chief concern is how God used this human being Jesus, this son of Adam who was God's only Son, to save a sinful humanity. Neither the first father of our race nor his offspring could achieve it, for "it was not possible for the man who had once for all been conquered, and who had been destroyed by disobedience, to reform himself, and obtain the prize of victory. . . ."[1] One stronger than Satan was required to overcome the enslaver of our race. Jesus was that person. "Who else is superior to, and more eminent than, that man who was formed after the likeness of God, except the Son of God, after whose image humanity was created?"[2]

Although Jesus was the Son of God, it was precisely in his humanness that he won the victory for us. He professed himself the Son of man, Irenaeus says, in order that, "as our species went down to death through a vanquished human, so we may ascend to life again through a victorious one; and, as through a human, death received the palm of victory against us, so again by a human we may receive the palm against death."[3]

The Incarnate Son — Greek Style

The Jesus of the patristic period is always the incarnate Son, the Christ of faith. This does not keep its writers from describing him richly. For Clement of Alexandria he is "the Lord Jesus, who by the will of the Almighty is 'the overseer of our hearts' (1 Pet. 2:25), whose blood was consecrated for us."[4] "As the sun . . . sends its rays through windows and small chinks into the furthest recesses of a house, so the Word, poured out everywhere, beholds the smallest actions of human lives."[5] "He was despised for his appearance, but is worshiped for his work; he is the purifying, saving, delectable Word, the divine Word, who is truly God most manifest, made equal to the Ruler of all; because he was the son, and 'the Word was with God.'"[6]

There is a special twist given to the portrait of Jesus by this Clement, which bears no relation to his failure to be reckoned a "church father." The latter judgment came from a few imaginative, indeed venturesome positions that later did not prove to be the church's faith. The special feature we refer to is part of the Greek philosophical tendency that saw human perfection as progress toward *apatheia*, a transcendence of all desires and impulses. Many Greek writers could hail the magnificence of Jesus in the following way, which would have left the Jews who knew him in his lifetime speechless:

> He ate, not because of bodily needs — since his body was supported by holy power, but so that his companions might not entertain a false notion about him . . . namely, that he had been manifested only in appearance. He himself was, and remained, "untroubled by passion (*apathēs*)"; no movement of the passions, either pleasure or pain, found its way into him.[7]

This shows that the very features that would have established his perfect human nature to Jews, his lively passions, were considered nonindications of the same in the Stoic way of thinking. For the Greeks, in Jesus' freedom from passionate nature lay the perfection of his humanity. God was conceived in quite the same way by the Greek mind. The perfection of deity consisted in the divine incapacity to undergo change. As to Jesus Christ, "[as Word] he remains unchanged in his essential being *(ousia)* while he descends to take part in human affairs by the providence and dispensation [of God]." Thus writes Origen in *Against Celsus* (IV, 14). There is no need to spell out how influential this kind of thinking has been in the church. It is defensibly Johannine, but it is surely at odds with most of the other descriptions of Jesus found in the Christian Scriptures.

At the same time, neither Origen nor any writer whose views were largely on the side of "orthodoxy" wished to dispute the clear gospel record:

> [In the agony in Gethsemane] he displays, in his human nature, both the weaknesses of human flesh and the willingness of spirit: weakness in "Father, if it is possible let this cup pass from me"; willingness of spirit in "But not as I will, as you will."[8]

The reality of Jesus' having experienced "every temptation by which human beings are tempted" is allowed "for this purpose, that we might overcome through his victory. . . . It is clear that it was not God but man who was tempted."[9] That our Lord did not know "the day or the hour" is acknowledged a little less graciously, with explanations like the necessity of the consummation of all things in time before Christ's appointed work was completed, or his not knowing the day of final judgment in the sense that he will know it only when "the church, which is his body, knows it."[10]

Much attention was given in the patristic age to resisting the Arians, who thought that the eternal Word was a creature. Hence, while the humanity of Jesus was granted, it was done in such a way that the divine power of the Word was immediately proposed as the force behind it. "No one should feel perplexed at hearing of birth, body, passions and death being thus referred to the immaterial and incorporeal Word of God," writes Eusebius of Caesarea (d. ca. 339) in his *Demonstration of the Gospel.*[11] He assures the reader that the incorporeal power of God suffers nothing in its essence when it comes in contact with a corporeal substance. The divine Word, writes Eusebius,

> called people and healed them freely by means of the human instrument which had been brought into being, just as a musician shows skill by means of the lyre. Like a good doctor, he gave to sick souls in human bodies the right and appropriate help — the help of his humanity."[12]

Eusebius in the same treatise says that the Word swallows up the humanity of Jesus in its entirety upon his glorification, "thereby giving us all the perfect exemplar of what it will be to share his immortality and to reign at his side."

The Eusebian thinking about Christ was, by a later, Chalcedonian standard, somewhat confused. A discourse on the feast of the Nativity *(Sermon 28)* by Leo I, bishop of Rome, is by contrast filled with clear distinctions on the mystery directed against a variety of heretics, as we might expect from the author of the *Tome* on which the definition of Chalcedon (A.D. 451) was based:

> In celebrating our Lord and Savior's birthday . . . we must have a complete and true conception of the childbearing of the blessed Virgin. We must believe that there was no moment of time at which the power of the Word was absent from the flesh and soul that were conceived. . . . There was one Son of God and of man, in whom the divinity was without mother and the humanity without father. By the Holy Spirit a virgin was made fruitful, and without trace of corruption gave birth at one and the same moment to the offspring and founder of the race.

The above excerpt highlights a set of paradoxes that could be culled from hundreds of sermons of the high patristic period: that is, the limitations of humanity set free by the marvel of deity, deity confined by the free option to take on humanity—

but without distinction or division in the one person who was Jesus Christ.

"He Humbled Himself . . ."

A theology of the hypostatic union (two natures in one *hypostasis* or "subsistence," the divine Word) was identified chiefly with Alexandria, a theology of the indwelling Word with Antioch. The West's distinctive contribution was the idea of *kenōsis* or "emptying" (cf. Phil. 2:7), developed chiefly by Hilary of Poitiers. Augustine and Leo later featured it, making kenotic theology the backbone of the compromise represented by the decree of Chalcedon. "We were raised because he was lowered" is the way Hilary described the exchange that was its underlying soteriology. "Shame to him was glory to us. He, being God, made flesh his residence, and we in return are lifted anew from the flesh to God."[13] By Christ's humiliation he taught the human race humility so that it could be exalted with him.

This christology of pre-existence, emptying, and exaltation was not worked out very precisely, but it satisfied the requirements of the West which were less demanding theologically than those of the East. Leo in writing his *Tome to Flavian* inclined more to the Antiochean than the Alexandrian position, but he is as strong as one could wish on the unity of Christ's person (without the hypostatic union of Cyril of Alexandria). He tells all the stories of the gospels while keeping in balance Jesus' "being pierced with nails and opening the gates of Paradise to the faith of the thief."[14] The stress, despite the balance, is on "lowliness assumed by majesty, weakness by power, mortality by eternity" *(ibid., 3)*.

The net effect of this kenotic emphasis was a christology in the West that took the form chiefly of a compassion for the weak and suffering Jesus Christ. His was a divine power that chose not to express itself fully. He would vindicate a suffering humanity in its resurrection to glory in the same way that he was raised up by the power of God made manifest in him.

Jesus as Lovable

Saint Augustine was, of course, the great popularizer of this
view. He fixed firmly in the consciousness of the West the importance of Jesus Christ in the life of the believer. The preachers
and theologians of a thousand years were the spiritual heirs
of Augustine.

There follows a selection from this church father which
is representative of hundreds such scattered throughout his
writings:

> For inasmuch as he was born of a mother who . . . al-
> though always a virgin . . . was yet married to a worker,
> he put an end to the inflated pride of worldly respectabil-
> ity. He was born in the town of Bethlehem . . . so that
> no one could glory in the importance of an earthly city.
> He to whom all things belong and by whom all things
> were created became poor, lest anyone believing in him
> should dare to be unduly exalted because of this world's
> riches. . . . He hungered who feeds all, he thirsted by
> whom all drink is created. . . . He was wearied by earthly
> journeying who has made himself the way to heaven for
> us. . . . He was bound who has freed people from the
> bonds of their infirmities. . . .[15]

The Italian archbishop of Canterbury, Anselm of Bec (d.
1109)— despite his spare philosophical argumentation in the
Monologion and *Proslogion* — could write this prayer to Jesus
Christ seven centuries later because all Latin-speaking Europe
bore Augustine's kenotic stamp:

> Kindest, gentlest, most serene Lord,
> will you not make it up to me for not seeing
> the blessed incorruption of your flesh,
> for not having kissed the place of the wounds
>   where the nails pierced,
> for not having sprinkled with tears of joy
> the scars that prove the truth of your body? . . .
>   Alas, Lord, alas, my soul.

You have ascended, consoler of my life,
and you have not said farewell to me. . . .
    "Lifting up your hands"
you were received by a cloud into heaven,
    and I did not see it;
angels promised your return; and I did not hear it.[16]

This warmhearted, direct mode of address to the suffering Jesus had not characterized the fathers of the church, even
though the commentaries of Gregory the Great, Aponius, and
Isidore on the *Canticle* (as they called it in Latin) represented
a certain breakthrough. These patristic treatises on the *Song
of Songs* placed the believer figuratively in the position of the
pining female lover and Christ in the role of the beloved. We
find the usage in the prayer of Anselm just quoted from, amidst
a tissue of biblical quotations:

Where shall I seek him? Where and when shall I find him?
    Whom shall I ask? Who shall tell me of my beloved?
        "for I am sick from love". . . .
Come now, Lord, appear to me and I will be consoled;
    show me your face and I shall be saved;
        display your presence and I will have obtained my
            desire. . . .
"My soul thirsts for you, my flesh longs after you." . . .
My consoler, for whom I wait, when will you come?[17]

Christ the Bridegroom

This effusive address of the Christian to Christ, made indis-
criminately by a male or female devotee, was to mark the entire medieval period in the West. In it Jesus is conceived of
as the strong male lover or, for propriety's sake, the groom,
while the believer or the whole church is the bride (cf. 2 Cor.
11:2; Eph. 5:25-27). In the twelfth century there is a great upsurge of attention to the *Canticle*, beginning with Anselm of
Laon (whose commentary was later attributed to Anselm of
Bec) and culminating in the eighty-six sermons of Bernard of

Clairvaux (d. 1153) on it. Bernard's interpretation was, overtly, thoroughly asexual and saw in the male and female figures the divine Word and a questing soul.

Apart from his harsh and ascetical temperament, Bernard was perhaps also motivated by his antipathy to his archrival, Abelard (d. ca. 1142). Abelard, a tonsured cleric and peripatetic teacher, had taken his pleasure with his young student Heloise (d. 1164) and then married her, following which they separated and repaired to monasteries for the rest of their days. Abelard's letters to her thereafter, filled with a penitent spirit, write of Jesus as he had not been thought of in the previous centuries:

> Are you not moved to tears or remorse by the only be-
> gotten Son of God who, for you and for all humanity,
> in his innocence was seized by the hands of impious men,
> dragged along and scourged, blindfolded, mocked at . . .
> finally hanged between thieves on the cross . . .? Think
> of him always, sister, as your true spouse and as the
> spouse of all the church. Keep him in mind. Look at him
> going to be crucified for your sake. . . .[18]

In another letter to Heloise on the origin of nuns, Abelard explores the gospel data on the special attention Jesus paid to women, among them Mary of Bethany, Mary Magdalene, and the woman who poured ointment on his head.[19] His mother, Mary, Elizabeth, the Samaritan woman, and the women who petitioned him for cures are all there. What seems a common-place to us was in fact uncommon for the times: a careful cata-logue of Jesus' relation as a male to those of the female sex. It simply had not been usual to explore his human reactions to the people around him. Abelard does just as well in examin-ing the detachment from possessions of monastic life, saying as he tracked down the various counsels of the gospels: "In forsaking everything we follow naked a naked Christ, as the holy apostles did."[20] He then proceeds to apply the teachings of Jesus on the renunciation of family attachments and even of self to the specifics of monastic existence.

Jesus Suffering for Us

The twelfth century saw a number of women mystics, most of them members of Saint Bernard's Cistercian order, whose piety was centered on the passion of Christ. Elizabeth of Schönau had her brother Eckbert record her *Visio*[21] in which she saw the cross of Jesus glowing with shafts of light on the feast of its Exaltation. Visions 55 and 56 make up a long meditation on the passion of Christ, from the kiss of Judas to the earthquake after the crucifixion. "My pain is nothing compared to Christ's pain," she exclaims at one point as she records her visions, feeling her heart become liquid and "almost stolen away in rapture."

Saint Lutgard was another Cistercian of the twelfth century—the first saint to participate in the mystical exchange of hearts with Christ. She experienced the *stigma* of the spear wound of Jesus and frequently experienced his bloody sweat. The passion piety of this age seemed closely related to the Albigensian or Cathar heresy. Not only did Catholics take on themselves vicarious sufferings patterned on those of the Lord to make reparation for it, they also seem to have featured sexual and conjugal images of the soul's union with Christ to combat the heretical denial of the goodness of sex and childbearing.

Jesus as Mother

The tendency outlined above has been seen as part of a "feminine" or "affective" spirituality, but neither of these adjectives is quite accurate. Hildegard of Bingen appears to be the only female writer of the twelfth century to use maternal imagery when speaking of God or Christ. At the same time, the language patterns of this century began to employ emphasis on breasts and nurturing, the womb, conception, and union as incorporation. The chief male writers to speak in this way were Bernard, Aelred of Rievaulx, Isaac of Stella, William of

Saint-Thierry, and Anselm. Here is Anselm in a "Prayer to St. Paul":

> And you, Jesus, are you not also a mother?
> Are you not the mother who, like a hen,
> gathers her chickens under her wings?
> Truly, Lord, you are a mother;
> for both they who are in labour
> and they who are brought forth
> are accepted by you. . . .
> For, longing to bear offspring into life,
> you tasted of death,
> and by dying you begot them. . . .
> Christ, my mother,
> you gather your chickens under your wings;
> this dead chicken of yours puts himself under those
> wings.[22]

Saint Bernard writes in a letter: "If you feel the stings of temptation, . . . suck not so much the wounds as the breasts of the Crucified. He will be your mother and you will be his son."[23] Guerric, abbot of Igny (d. ca. 1157), says, similarly: "The Bridegroom . . . has breasts lest he should be lacking any one of all the duties and titles of loving kindness. . . . He is mother in the mildness of his affection, and a nurse."[24] Aelred of Rievaulx (in England; pronounced "Rivers") meditates more on the infancy and childhood of Jesus but he too has the image of "his naked breasts [which] will feed you with the milk of sweetness to console you."[25] This lactation figure is prominent probably because the physiology of the age thought that this milk was processed blood. Adam, abbot of Perseigne (d. 1221), refers Jesus' image of labor pains (John 16:21) to the Lord himself as he begets us.

Where did these twelfth-century motifs originate? Were they part of a new appreciation of the feminine and motherhood in that age, an attempt to restore the longstanding imbalance of male figures for God? Probably not. It is quite likely that the above monastic writers, all of them abbots, were burdened by the necessity of being father, mother, and all to their monks and, at times, to the nuns they gave spiritual direction to. In a preindustrial society, breastfeeding was universal and childbearing a fact of universal male experience. Jesus hence became a womb and breasts and a mother's love because the onerous office of abbot required that the abbot be such in this all-male society. In any event, we have the beginnings of a new tenderness in the Western image of Jesus.

The Difference
Francis of Assisi
Made

The appreciation of Jesus that was special to Saint Francis brought about an immense change in the piety of the West, indeed of anyone on the globe who encountered the saint's thought or example. Most people who know fragments of the life of this *poverello* as he called himself — "little poor one" — recognize in him authentic discipleship of Jesus of Nazareth. They see in Francis a total fidelity to the call of Jesus, the artisan who deserted a comfortable village existence for the open road without a place to lay his head.

Many before Saint Francis, born Giovanni Bernardone, had followed Jesus and the gospel in their state — as devout peasants, as nobility, as hermits, or as sharers in a common monastic life. The man of Assisi did not devise the mendicant life of the itinerant friar. Neither did Domingo de Guzmán, who was older than Francis and whose rule was formally approved earlier. Both saints, however, played a central part in a movement of their age.

It was Francis who brought this movement to a peak, which soon after his death became a crisis. He confronted institutional Catholic life with the challenge of living absolutely without possessions in the service of the gospel. Papacy, bishopric, and corporately wealthy monasticism had to come to terms with the reform he represented. (The village clergy had no great problem, being by and large as poor as he. But their poverty was involuntary and hence often grudging, besides being hedged in by a frightful ignorance.) The preaching brothers of Francis prevailed in the struggle, but barely. They institutionalized a detachment from possessions without insisting (as some of his early followers did) that if one owned anything, one could not call oneself a Christian.

Toward Imitating Jesus' Life

Central to the vision of Francis was the decision to imitate the life of the Poor Man of Nazareth. Monks and nuns had long attempted this by rule and vow, but social structures like landholding and landlording got in the way. In the last chapter we examined briefly the new trend of personal piety of the twelfth-century Cistercians, themselves a reform movement of the "black monks" of Saint Benedict. This trend incorporated a commitment of the feelings and emotions to Jesus, the incarnate Son of the gospels — the first three gospels especially — which had not marked the previous centuries. The Jesus of their concern was a compassionate doer on humanity's behalf, and not only in his final hours of the passion and cross. The abbots of the tradition of Citeaux, and some monks and nuns they directed, began to address Jesus warmly in the terms of the beloved addressing the lover in the Song of Songs. Affections were displayed in religious writing that had not previously been

given voice. The institution of knighthood and the conceit of
courtly love were probably influential in this development.
The monks and nuns were, after all, often the sons and daugh-
ters of the nobility for whom no advantageous marriage could
be arranged. Their natural hungers of the heart were sublimated
in a romance with the divine Spouse. He was an idealized
Christ, a "Lord of heaven," but the gospels were at the same
time pored over for Jesus' earthly expressions of love and
service with which both sexes could identify.

The general lines of the life of Saint Francis are too well
known to rehearse in detail: the gaudy dress of his youth which
earned him the sobriquet that stuck, "the Frenchman"; the
acquisition of a poor man's rags in exchange for his own which,
with a rope at the waist, he never deserted; the vision experienced in a tiny deserted chapel, with the spoken injunction
of Jesus: "Francis, restore my house"; the wounds of Christ
received on the heights of La Verna; the leper embraced, the
birds homilized, the wolf subdued.

Some of these stories about Saint Francis are well-known
tales of the postmorten *Fioretti*, a garland of remembrances
in which the lilies were often gilded. Others are found in the
soberer account by his first official biographer, Buonaventura
of Bagnorea — an account that was officially commissioned
by the friars who outlived the founder. It bore the title *Legenda
Maior*, the "longer reading," and was artfully composed from
two earlier "Lives" by Thomas of Celano plus his tractate on
miracles and another "life" by Julian of Speyer. Some portions
derive from none of these sources. Buonaventura, or Saint
Bonaventure, says he visited the sites of Francis's birth, life,
and death, carefully interviewing his companions, and decided
to write it all up in simple, not ornate style. The product is
a marvelous tissue of apposite quotations from the Bible, an
edifying account that is not free of legends but is realistic in
its overall effect. It makes of Francis a Paul-like figure in his
mission; for example: "He seemed like a mother who was
daily in labor pains, bringing them to birth in Christ."[1] We do

not know how "Pauline" Francis was in his preaching. We do know that he restored the image of the Jesus of the gospels to European consciousness through the heritage he gave his preaching friars. "He was *poor and lowly*," Bonaventure writes, "but *the Most High God looked upon* him with such condescension and kindness that he not only *lifted him up . . . from the dust* of a worldly life, but made him a practitioner, a leader and a herald of Gospel perfection" (*Legenda*, prologue; biblical portions italicized).

Literally Imitating Jesus

Saint Francis was also part of a movement other than that of itinerant mendicancy. There was in the lecture halls of Paris toward the end of his short life (he was dead by the age of forty-five) a departure from the "spiritual interpretation" of the Bible that had prevailed from the church fathers through Saint Bernard of Clairvaux. In place of this symbolic reading calculated to lift the heart to divine things came a literal sense based on a knowledge of secular philosophy. William of Auvergne, bishop of Paris shortly after Francis's death in 1226, was the pioneer in this. In William's lectures the traditional search for moralities and doctrines in Scripture continued but, aided by Arabic and Greek learning, he also tracked down the meaning of the letter. Saint Dominic's Friars Preachers led the movement in the schools. The "little brothers" of Francis did the same in the town squares. Both in halls of learning and in the open air, "the old allegories and moralities were fading before an intense realization of the literal meaning."[2]

Thus, Saint Francis attempted to imitate Jesus as literally as possible. A novice once asked Francis for a book of psalms, and he replied that he, too, had once been tempted to desire books but then opened the gospels to learn God's will in the matter. His eye fell on Matt. 13:11 where Jesus tells his disciples that it is given to them to know the mysteries of the kingdom. This he took immediately to be a command to poverty and simplicity. This narrative comes from an early Franciscan document called *Intentio Regulae*. A person of a century before would have seen in this text an invitation to pursue the mystical meaning of Scripture. Francis saw in it the strictest literal understanding. Consequently, he led his friars to seek a sharing in the sufferings of Jesus. In this new historical approach, "What is evoked by the crib, the rosary, the crucifix [new devotions of the age], is the Gospel in its literal sense."[3]

Imitating the Suffering Jesus

Francis acquired a little knowledge of reading and writing in his youth, Bonaventure writes, then gave himself to his father's "lucrative merchant's business." Despite the companionship of wealthy young men like himself, he never gave himself up to greed or sexual pleasures. An encounter with a destitute knight triggered for him a dream in which he saw himself, Quixote-like, taking horse to defend helpless women in distress and the poor. Francis got a day's journey away from Assisi, intending to hire himself out to a local count, when he heard the voice of Jesus say to him by night: "Why are you deserting the Lord for a servant and the rich God for a poor man?" Thinking this a bad bargain, Francis dropped out of the world of trade and asked God what the divine good pleasure for him might be.

The encounter with a desperately afflicted man was the turning point: "When the leper put out his hand as if to receive some alms, Francis gave him money and a kiss. . . . From that time on he clothed himself with a spirit of poverty . . . visited the houses [of lepers] frequently, generously distributing alms to them and with great compassion kissed their hands and their mouths. To beggars he wished to give not only his compassion but his very self."[4]

The motivation in all this was a desire to emulate Jesus in the spirit of Is. 53:3-4, a passage in which a mysterious servant of the LORD is "despised . . . smitten by God, and afflicted." Bonaventure says in summary, 'Francis, the servant of the Most High, had no other teacher in these matters except Christ."[5]

There came a violent break with his father, followed by the physical repair of three churches successively. He began living among lepers, dressing their wounds as he awaited some heavenly sign of his next move. He received it with the proclamation of that gospel portion at Mass where Jesus tells his disciples that they "should not keep gold or silver or money in their belts, nor have a wallet for the journey, nor two tunics, nor shoes, nor staff" (Matt. 10:9-10). From then on Francis "tried to conform in every way to the rule of right living given to the apostles."[6] He began to gather companions — seven in all, one a local priest — and to preach, an activity that was totally unassociated with laymen of his day. The theme of all his preaching was the proclamation of peace. As he put it, in imitation of Jesus, "May the Lord give you peace" (Matt. 10:13; Luke 10:5).

As the number of his "brothers" grew he wrote them a simple rule. He then went off to Rome to ask Pope Innocent III to approve it. Luckily, the pope was a reformer himself, but he at first held back "because it seemed to some of the cardinals to be something novel and difficult beyond human powers."[7] A pious one among the cardinals removed the pope's scruple, abetted by a parable Francis told Innocent about his "little Order" as a "poor mother." Francis's rule was approved in 1220 and a second, shorter version by Honorius III in 1223. Both were simplicity itself, inviting the brothers and *pauperes dominae* ("poor ladies," popularly "Clares") to share in the humility, the poverty, and the sufferings of Christ.

Nowhere in Bonaventure's life is Francis remembered as lugubrious, or a "downer"; rather he is always depicted as a joyful spirit whose early desire to be a troubadour or minstrel was never dimmed. He lived a life of extreme bodily austerity, "calling his body Brother Ass, for he felt it should be subjected to heavy labor, beaten frequently with whips and fed with the poorest food."[8] One hopes that this sentiment contains more of the religious rhetoric of the times than the sober truth. The same should be said of his view of woman, whom he seemed to think the celibate could only recognize as temptress.[9] It is by no means easy at this distance to know what is meant by "following the spotless crucified Lamb so perfectly as to avoid contacting any filth" (this sentiment not in a sexual connection), for which he prescribed cleansing with streams of tears.

A Jesus for the Suffering and Oppressed

While Francis saw in the "most holy life of Christ the model of perfection," Bonaventure nowhere indicates that the Lord's resurrection was the subject of the saint's contemplation. In the spirit of the times it was probably subsumed under a lively hope of heaven, where the Savior is in glory. But of references to Jesus' victory over death there is nothing. Life as a succession of vain deluding pleasures can only be countered by repentance and suffering. Even the evangelist Mark, the first to foster a piety of the cross, did better than Francis in his threefold prediction of the resurrection and his concluding: "He is risen, he is not here. . . . Go, tell his disciples and Peter that he is going to Galilee before you" (16:6-7).

The Poverello should not be charged with major default. It was enough that he restored to Europe, and through it to parts of Asia and Africa, a lively awareness of the human side of the incarnation — a "God with us" in Jesus Christ, with whom great populations of the suffering and oppressed could identify. The incarnation was a self-imposed humiliation of God for Saint Francis — not in the spirit of the christology of Philippians 2 but as a window on the divine compassion. That God through the Son should do this, endure this for me, was his constant cry. What the enthroned King of Glory had done for the landless peasantry of the patristic age the disenfranchised Lord of heaven did for a feudal age. Popes, kings, bishops, barons too — the last classes from whom to expect poverty of fact — took on not only the Franciscan spirit but the Franciscan reality. They looked within, they wept, and — greatest marvel of all — in modest numbers they adopted the poverty of Jesus.

Like a man of his time, Saint Francis often employed the rhetoric of the military to describe spiritual things. At the same time he so brought the peace-loving Jesus to the fore that he gave an embattled medieval world a commitment to peace it had not known. He did not stop wars or crusades, but he did help put all of Christian Europe in bad faith over its offended "honor," routine feuds, and cruel bloodletting. He records in his *Testament* that he learned the greeting *"May the Lord give you peace"* in a revelation from the Lord himself. Bonaventure says he never failed to give it as a greeting to the people at the beginning of his sermons. He did more. "By his salutary warnings he united in a bond of true peace many who had previously been in opposition to Christ and far from salvation."[10] There is no mention in the gospels of Jesus' respect for all of life like that of the Hindu saints, but Francis extended the Christ-like peace he proclaimed to a love of every creature, even the gnats and the bees. His gentleness, no less than his strength of character, was universal.

The devotion of Saint Francis to the infancy of Jesus spread as widely as his devotion to the cross. The following account of the origins of the *crèche* (from the town of Greccio), found in chapter 10 of the *Legenda*, seems important enough to be given in its entirety:

> It happened in the third year before his death [1223] that he decided, in order to arouse devotion, to celebrate at Greccio with the greatest possible solemnity the memory of the birth of the Child Jesus. So that this would not be considered a type of novelty, he petitioned for and obtained permission from the Supreme Pontiff. He had a crib prepared, hay carried in and an ox and ass led to the place. The friars are summoned, the people come, the forest resounds with their voices and that venerable night

is rendered brilliant and solemn by a multitude of bright
lights and by resonant and harmonious hymns of praise.
The man of God stands before the crib, with Francis as
deacon [he was never in priest's orders] chanting the holy
Gospel. Then he preaches to the people standing about
concerning the birth of the poor King, whom, when he
wished to name him, he called in his tender love, the
Child of Bethlehem.

Crucified with Jesus

The opposite pole on the axis of Franciscan devotion, as it
became the heritage of the West, is the account of his receiv-
ing the imprint of Jesus' wounds on Mount La Verna. It occurs
in chapter 13 of the *Legenda*. Saint Bonaventure describes him
as customarily leaving the restlessness of the crowds to seek
out solitude, there to "spend his time more freely with the
Lord." Two years before his death he was one day *"led apart*
by divine providence to a *high* place" where, "according to
his usual custom, he had begun to fast for forty days in honor
of St. Michael the Archangel (viz., from August 15 to
September 29, the 'Lent of St. Michael')." There,

> on a certain morning about the feast of the Exaltation
> of the Cross [September 14], while Francis was praying
> on the mountainside, he saw a Seraph with six fiery and
> shining wings descend from the height of heaven. And
> when in swift flight the Seraph had reached a spot in the
> air near the man of God, there appeared between the
> wings the figure of a man crucified, with his hands and
> feet extended in the form of a cross and fastened to a
> cross. . . . Eventually he understood by a revelation from
> the Lord that divine providence had shown him this
> vision so that, as Christ's lover, he might learn in advance
> that he was to be totally transformed into the likeness
> of Christ crucified, not by the martyrdom of his flesh,
> but by the fire of love consuming his soul.
>
> As the vision disappeared, it left in his heart a mar-
> velous ardor and imprinted on his body markings that

were no less marvelous. Immediately the marks of nails began to appear in his hands and feet just as he had seen a little before in the figure of the man crucified. . . . Also his right side, as if pierced with a lance, was marked with a red wound from which his sacred blood often flowed, moistening his tunic and underwear.

Francis came down from the mountain at the end of his forty-day vigil, "bearing with him the image of the Crucified, which was depicted not on *tablets of stone* or on panels of wood by the hand of a craftsman, but engraved in the members of his body *by the finger of the living God.*"[11]

The imprint of the Poverello has been made upon Catholic Europe in the seven centuries since his time just as clearly as the *stigmata* ("marks") of Christ were made upon Francis. He introduced into Catholic life an intimacy with the person of the man Jesus to which the gospels invited Christians but which the doctrinal settlements of the patristic age tended to discourage. Identification with the Lord in every phase of his human life became central to the piety of the West through Francis. The doctrinal struggles of the Reformation did nothing to dislodge this passion piety in particular — rather, the contrary was the case. Saint Francis survived as the one authentic Protestant saint not mentioned in the Bible, chiefly because he pointed unerringly to the need for the devoted and undiluted following of Christ. Even his devotion to the Blessed Virgin Mary was forgiven him by the Reformers.

His desire for martyrdom led him to Egypt and an audience with the sultan during the fifth crusade, which was then being fought near Cairo. The exchange was inconclusive. The sultan's amazement at such simplicity and faith is the chief reaction recorded. What came of the failed attempt to preach Christ to him was the peaceful presence of the friars in Muslim lands and the custody of the "holy places" there over many centuries. This close conjunction of the friars with the places where Jesus lived and taught is a logical outcome of the near-total identification of the "little poor one" with the Savior.

Some Medieval English Mystics

We have seen in previous chapters the upsurge of affective writing with Jesus at its center in twelfth-century France and the Low Countries, then the spread of Jesus piety in the thirteenth century through the efforts of Saint Francis and his "little brothers." We turn now to a development in fourteenth-century England that would have had a far greater influence on us if "Mary's Dowry" — as that country liked to call itself in the Middle Ages — had remained Catholic. As things stand, the English mystics have begun to be reclaimed in the twentieth century by Catholics and perhaps even more by Anglicans. The latter is true, at least, in the universities and centers of piety, old-style.

"An Affection Unbounded"

The first of these contemplatives chronologically was Richard Rolle (pronounced like the name Raleigh) who was born in

Yorkshire about 1300. He did some university studies at Oxford in his late teens, left home to become a do-it-yourself hermit, and over the next three decades produced a stream of poetry and prose in English and Latin without benefit of holy orders or the customary license as a hermit. Rolle's best-known work is *The Fire of Love*, which we have in translation from the original *De Incendio Amoris*. This treatise, like all his writing, is highly emotive. He seems to have been a scrappy lot, often at odds with those of his contemporaries who were likewise engaged in spiritual direction and writing.

> Lift the lid of the pan, and there is only stink! Those who speak evil speak out of the abundance of their heart, and there lurks the poison of asps! I know this: the more men have been furious with me with their denigrations, the more have I advanced in spiritual growth. My worst detractors have been those I once counted my faithful friends.[1]

One is tempted to remark, *Ad astra per aspera!* But Rolle proves considerably more attractive in his total output than might be deduced from the above. Before his early death he persuaded some Cistercian nuns in a monastery near Doncaster — best known in modern times for its racecourse — to call on him as their spiritual director. From shortly after his death at age forty-nine until the onset of the Reformation he was venerated as "Saint Richard, Hermit."

Rolle does not provide any special insights into the person and character of Jesus. His christology is of a thoroughly familiar kind, deriving from sources like the Athanasian Creed.[2] What we do have from him is testimony to his intense devotion to Jesus, whom he views quite as his contemporaries did. Rolle's quotations from the gospels and familiar catechetical sources bring no surprises. "There is nothing so sweet as loving Christ," he writes, "and because this is so let us not inquire too closely into matters we earthbound creatures cannot possibly understand. In the Father's home there will be

clearer light if we bring our whole heart to the task of loving
God."[3] And in another place: "I longed for the sweet delights
of eternity, and I gave my soul over to love Christ with every
ounce of my power."[4] He says he longs for death, not for its
own sake, "but for the Saviour's, my Jesus, on whom, once
I have got what I want from you, I hope to gaze eternally."[5]
Something of his exuberance can be deduced from the following
poetic snatch, one of many interspersed in his lively prose:

> I ask you, Lord Jesus,
>   to develop in me, your lover,
>   an immeasurable urge towards you,
>   an affection that is unbounded,
>   a longing that is unrestrained,
>   a fervour that throws discretion to the winds.[6]

His prayer must have been answered, for he writes of his
love for Jesus with a complete absence of restraint. Rolle's
respect for womanhood and the state of marriage is not great.
Perhaps this is rhetorical in him as part of his effort to remain
chaste in his celibate state. But this stance must have been a
sublimation of desires in a man who could write:

> He who delights to do what his Saviour wishes, not
> surprisingly finds delight in this present world as well.
> Nothing is more pleasant than praising Jesus; nothing
> more delectable than hearing him. . . . When I feel the
> embrace and caress of my Sweetheart I swoon with
> unspeakable delight, for it is he — he whom true lovers
> put before all else, for love of him alone, and because
> of his unbounded goodness![7]

This extravagant prose, inexplicable at one level apart from
Freudian categories, is better understood if the two phrases
from the *Canticle of Canticles* are seen as the brackets within
which the passage falls: "*Let him kiss me with the kiss of his
mouth.* . . . in other words, let him delight me in union with
his Son. Faint with love, I long with my whole heart to see
my Love in all his beauty"; and, at the close: "We will rejoice as

we remember *your breasts that are better than wine,* as if to say, 'We are wanting your honour, your glory: / we are rejoicing in your delights.'"[8]

These passages tell us much about the spiritual and literary conceits of the age. They do not tell us much about Jesus except that he was viewed as the object of the most intense human affection. The soul speaks: "Let my Beloved kiss me and refresh me with his sweet love; let him hold me tight and kiss me on the mouth, else I die; let him pour his grace into me, that I may grow in love."[9] Flights of imagery like this abound in *The Fire of Love.* It would be tedious to multiply them. It would also be erroneous to take their sexual imagery literally, for it is entirely doubtful that a medieval like Rolle did. Jesus is simply the object of every human longing in a way that earthly pleasures and unlawful desires are not.

> *Go forth, daughters of Sion,* . . . meaning "you souls who are newborn," *and see King Solomon crowned,* meaning "understand Christ is truly our peace, for he suffered for our salvation. Gaze at him, and you will see that divine head crowned with thorns, his face spit-covered, those clear eyes languid and wan, his back scarred with flogging, his breast bare and bleeding. . . . Leave, then, leave your illicit lusts, and see what Christ has suffered for you, so that your sins can clearly be cast away, and your hearts taught to burn with love."[10]

"Never Cease of Ghostly Desiring"

Walter Hilton (d. 1396) and the anonymous author of *The Cloud of Unknowing* came in the generation after Rolle and refined his thought while not creating any new patterns of thought. Thus, Hilton could write in his *Scale of Perfection* (in fourteenth-century speech that is here modified but not made modern):

> I shall tell one word for all which thou shalt seek, desire, and find, for in that word is all that thou hast lost. This

word is Jesus. I mean not this word Jesus painted upon the wall, or written with letters upon the book, or formed by lips in sound of the mouth, nor feigned in thine heart by travail of thy mind; for on this manner wise, may a man of charity find him. But I mean Jesus Christ, that blessed person, God and Man, son of the Virgin Mary, whom this name betokeneth; that is all goodness, endless wisdom, love and sweetness, thy joy, thy worship, and thine everlasting bliss, thy God, thy Lord, and thy salvation.

Then by what manner prayer or meditation or occupation that thou mayest have great desire to him, and have most feeling of him, by that occupation, thou seest him best and best findest him. . . . And though it be so that thou feel him in devotion or in knowing . . . rest not therein as though thou hadst fully found Jesus; but forget that thou hadst found, and aye be desiring after Jesus more and more, for to find him better, as though thou hadst not right found him. . . . Know thou or feel thou ever so mickle [much] of him, he is yet above it. And therefore if thou wilt fully find him as he is, in the bliss of loving, cease never whilst thou livest of ghostly desiring."[11]

"Good Jesus! Sweet Jesus!"

Such mystical fastening upon Jesus as the great sacrament of God, as seen in the passages above, is done by Hilton in myriad verbal ways. It is therefore somewhat refreshing to see his contemporary (a country pastor, it has been deduced, with many under his direction) write in a much homelier vein some time about 1375:

Sweet indeed was that love between our Lord and Mary [of Bethany]. Much love had she for him. Much more had he for her. Whoever would really understand what passed between him and her — not superficially, but as the Gospel story, which is never wrong, testifies — would find that her love for him is so heartfelt, that nothing

less than himself could satisfy her, nor keep her heart
from him. [12]

The author then establishes that he thought that this Mary was
the same as the Magdalene at the tomb of John 20:11-13, an
almost universal medieval supposition. This does nothing to
interfere with the beauty of his exploration of her state of heart.
She "would not be comforted by angels" — here the accounts
in John and the synoptics are conflated — "because she thought
that whoever was seeking the King of angels would not stop
for mere angels." [13] A similar attempt to plumb the feelings of
a gospel character, this time Jesus himself, occurs a few chapters
later. *The Cloud* has been maintaining that in the work of loving God one has "no time to consider who is friend or foe,
brother or stranger," even though at times everyone feels
greater love for some than others.

> This is only right, and for many reasons. Love asks just
> that. For Christ felt a deeper affection for John, and Mary,
> and Peter, than for many others. But when the soul is
> wholly turned to God all people are equally dear to him,
> for he then feels no other cause for loving than God him-
> self. . . . Christ is our head, we his limbs, if we abide
> in charity, and he who would be our Lord's perfect dis-
> ciple must strain every nerve and muscle of his soul in
> this spiritual work to save his earthly brothers and sisters,
> just as our Lord did with his body on the Cross. How
> does he do this? Not only for his friends, his nearest and
> dearest, but by and large for all mankind, without more
> attention to one than to another. For all who quit sin and
> ask God's mercy will be saved by reason of Christ's
> sufferings. [14]

The author's main conviction is that the urgent movement of love in us is wholly God's work. Our work as contemplatives — and it is a hard one — is to keep all God's creation,
insofar as it is sin-inducing, covered by a cloud of forgetting.
At the same time there is another cloud acting as an obstruc-
tion between the soul and God. "Hammer away at this high

cloud of unknowing [in which God is shrouded] — and take your rest later!"[15] Original sin has created a miasma of some of God's creatures or their deeds, seen and felt, which should be *under* individuals. Instead, creatures proudly push in *above* would-be contemplatives, coming between them and God.[16] At times God will inflame the actual bodies of devout servants enabling them out of an abundance of spiritual gladness to cry out: "Good Jesus!" "Sweet Jesus!" Because this impulse comes from within it is not to be resisted, but all other comforts and sweetness that come from without are to be suspected. The lowly movement of love within the heart, which *The Cloud* calls good will, is to be trusted and followed. It is the substance of all perfection.

When the author of *The Cloud* wishes to illustrate how it must be with "you actives" and "you contemplatives," he lingers on the Martha-Mary story for seven chapters (17-23). There he is marvelously at ease situating Jesus in the midst of people's lives and them in his. But mainly the author is warning against flights of fancy in those who presumptuously forget that a cloud of unknowing is set between them and God. Similarly, he uses the ascension story in Luke to good effect, but again to remind contemplatives of the limits put upon them. Perfection of spirit is poles apart from any physical movement or place.

> It might more reasonably be called a sudden "changing" rather than a movement. For in contemplative praying we should forget all about time and place and body. So be careful not to take the physical ascension of Christ as an example, so that you try to lift your imagination physically upwards, as if you climb past the moon! It cannot be so spiritually. . . . No one can [ascend to heaven like Christ] except God. . . . So leave such error alone. It cannot be so.[17]

This is all sound advice. It makes one wish that the author of *The Cloud* had attempted to base all states of love and prayer on gospel stories of Jesus and his friends, but he does not.

"Full of Joy, Familiar and Courteous"

An English mystic who comes closer to that Christ-centered ideal is Julian of Norwich, an anchoress or woman solitary, who died some time after 1416. She lived, accompanied by a female servant, in a cell adjoining the parish church of St. Julian at Norwich opposite an Augustinian friary. Little is known of her apart from what she tells in her "Shewings" (pronounced *show-ings*, meaning "revelations"), an account of thirteen visions experienced when she was "thirty and one half" years of age. She wrote them up twice — once shortly after the occurrence in 1373, in twenty-five brief chapters (the Short Text), then later in life in a more mature version both theologically and stylistically in eighty-six chapters (the Long Text). She had great feeling in her youth for the passion of Christ and prayed for more. She wished she had been at the foot of the cross with Mary Magdalene and Jesus' other lovers (cf. John 19:25). She asked for the Savior's bodily pains in the form of an illness. All this was granted to her, along with the wound of contrition, the wound of compassion, and the wound of longing for God. Coming close to death but, suddenly, "by God's secret doing," recovering, she was shown by "our Lord a spiritual sight of his familiar [i.e. familial] love":

> He is our clothing, for he is that love which wraps and enfolds us, embraces us and guides us, surrounds us for his love, which is so tender that he may never desert us.[18]

This passage is followed by the much quoted one about the hazelnut held in Julian's hand — a symbol of the whole creation, which God made and loves and preserves. "God wishes to be known, and it pleases him that we should rest in him; for all things which are beneath him are not sufficient for us."[19]

The young recluse was grateful for her visions, but she knew that if she paid attention to herself she was nothing at all. Julian was also canny enough to realize that all power in the church was in the hands of male, schooled clerics so she peppered her treatise with protestations of her female ignorance, weakness, and frailty. All of this is belied by the theological vigor of her prose. She hews to a familiar doctrinal line throughout but lets a few chips fly, the novelty of which cannot have escaped her inventive mind. She goes safely armored throughout by her ignorance and her frailty.

Her chief "showing" is of Jesus in his suffering: "I saw the body bleeding copiously, the blood hot, flowing freely, a living stream. . . . And I saw this in the furrows made by the scourging, and I saw this blood run so plentifully that . . . if it had been happening there . . . the bed and everything around it would have been soaked in blood."[20] She knows that the cause, not the pain, is of supreme moment here. The blessed blood has flowed to wash us of our sins. "With this the fiend is overcome," our Lord says to her in her soul, without voice and without opening of lips. The devil is the butt of God's sport and scorn and seriousness, overcome as he is "in great earnest and with heavy labour."[21]

Julian's descriptions of the suffering Jesus are extremely graphic but free of the usual clichés. The Long Text says at one point: "He was hanging up in the air as people hang up a cloth to dry."[22] She asks, concerning the passion: "Is there any pain in hell like this? And in my reason I was answered that despair is greater, for that is a spiritual pain."[23] Jesus in his agony is her heaven, "for I would rather have remained in that pain until Judgement Day than have come to heaven any other way than by him."[24]

What is remarkable about her description of Jesus' state in his passion is that he seems to confide in her how he devised and carried out the work of human salvation. "It was done as honourably as Christ could do it, and in this I saw complete joy in Christ; but his joy would not have been complete if the deed could have been done any better than it was."[25] "Are you well satisfied that I suffered for you?" he asks, and when she says yes: "It is a joy, a bliss, an endless delight that ever I suffered my Passion for you; and if I could suffer more,

I should suffer more."[26] His repeated watchword to her on the deed he has done in the face of sin, which is nothing, is "But all will be well, and all will be well, and every kind of thing will be well."[27]

There is no subject of Julian's visions except the suffering Jesus and yet the treatise is suffused with an unspeakable joy. He is "full of joy, familiar and courteous and blissful and true life."

> Again and again our Lord said: I am he, I am he. I am he who is highest. I am he whom you love. I am he in whom you delight. I am he whom you serve. I am he for whom you long. I am he whom you desire. I am he whom you intend. I am he who is all. I am he whom Holy Church preaches and teaches to you."[28]

When our courteous Lord shows himself to the soul he welcomes it as a courteous friend, as if it had been in pain and prison, saying:

> My dear darling, I am glad that you have come to me in all your woe. I have always been with you; and now you see me loving, and we are made one in bliss.[29]

There are a number of remarkable reflections in the Long Text (the work of Julian's maturity in 1393 or thereabouts). One is the claim in the forty-sixth chapter that — despite "the common teaching of Holy Church" (from which she is not moved or led away) that we deserve pain, blame, and wrath —

> I saw truly that our Lord was never angry, and never will be. Because he is God, he is good, he is truth, he is love, he is peace; and his power, his peace, his charity, his unity do not allow him to be angry. For I saw that it is against the property of his power to be angry. . . . God is that goodness which cannot be angry, for it is nothing but goodness. Our soul is united to him who is unchangeable goodness. And between God and our soul there is neither wrath nor forgiveness in his sight.[30]

Perhaps the best-known departure of Julian from common Christian speech is her easy description of both God and Christ as our true mother. William of Saint-Thierry seems to have done it before her in his Latin treatise in praise of contemplative life, *Golden Epistle*, but few have remarked on it. This seems to show the perils of writing in the vernacular and of being a woman. Julian begins her reflections traditionally enough. Our Lady is our mother. She is the mother of our Savior. She is the mother of all who are saved in our Savior. Pope Paul VI might have said as much. Then Julian writes: "And our saviour is our true Mother, in whom we are endlessly born and out of whom we shall never come."[31] Julian continues: "And so in our making, God almighty is our loving Father, and God all wisdom is our loving Mother. . . . In our almighty Father we have our protection and our bliss . . . our restoration and our salvation, for he is our Mother, brother and saviour."[32] She goes on:

> And furthermore I saw that the second person, who is our Mother, substantially the same beloved person, has now become our mother sensually, because we are double by God's creating, that is to say substantial and sensual.[33] Jesus Christ, who opposes good to evil, is our true Mother. We have our being from him, where the true foundation of motherhood begins, with all the sweet protection of love which endlessly follows."[34]

In excerpting from Julian of Norwich one has the uneasy feeling that all the wrong passages have been chosen. Has she been conveyed as offbeat, a dissident rather than the solid and traditional person she is? God is Holy Church, she likes to say, and she means it. But her visions have given her a freedom in that Church in which she basks and invites us to bask. She is graced with an uncommon word power that makes the English speaker exult in all that it can mean to be a Christian in this medium. Jesus suffers but he is never an object of pity. He is a conquerer carrying us along with him as he overcomes the nothingness of sin. He is as female as he is male, a person of breasts and womb, which begot and nurture and dandle us.

Most importantly of all, there are no heavenly icons on Julian's Olympus. There are people. God is people and so is Jesus Christ and so is the Holy Spirit. Julian speaks to them as they speak to us. Her prayer is a conversation. It is not a monologue directed at God.

We are the richer for these "shewings" of the pearl of East Anglia. Forthright, candid, a no-nonsense person, she is at the same time as tender and understanding as one could hope for. She convinces us that "our courteous Lord" is very much the same.[35]

6

Voices From the Troubled Times of the Renaissance and Reform

Desiderius Erasmus (1466-1536) was an Augustinian canon who spent very little time in the Dutch cloister of Steyn that claimed him, but he corresponded endlessly with his superiors to maintain his good standing as a cleric under vows. In 1516 this humanist scholar, patronized by the royal and academic establishments of continental Europe and England, was appointed chancellor to the Prince of Burgundy, who would later be the Emperor Charles V. One year later, 1517, he wrote a treatise in Latin entitled *Querela Pacis*, "The Complaint of Peace."

In those years the Turkish threat — the "Mahometans" as the English called them — was uppermost in the minds of Christian Europe, much as Russian Communism is in the West today. Then as now many people, even churchmen, supposed that anything was allowable ethically and even in one's state of heart with respect to this enemy of Christ and the gospel. Erasmus was shocked by the command of the otherwise admirable reformer, Cardinal Ximenez of Spain, issued to his galleys to approach the coasts of Africa and Italy — a warlike gesture from a representative of the Prince of Peace. Cardinal Wolsey was at the same time plotting a war policy for England which was not directly related to the Ottoman Turkish threat. In a year in which religious storm clouds were gathering (Luther would send the archbishop of Mainz his theses on 1 November), Erasmus wrote a treatise accusing fellow Christians in power of threatening the political peace by their un-Christian behavior. Peace is the speaker in this brief but powerful complaint of some thirty printed pages. Erasmus has her say:

> Men who are not ashamed to be called Christians act in total disagreement with what is most important to Christ. Consider his life. What is it other than a doctrine of concord and love? What do his commandments and parables teach? Peace and charity. Did the prophet Isaiah, when he foretold of the coming of Christ, promise that he should be a ruler of cities or warrior? No! What then did he promise? A Prince of Peace.[1]

The learned canon observes that as often as Holy Scripture indicates absolute happiness it does so under the name of peace. Whoever brings tidings of Christ brings tidings of peace, and whoever proclaims war proclaims him who is quite unlike Christ. The testy Dutchman then proceeds to cull from the gospels, chiefly that of John, the essence of Jesus of Nazareth as a peacemaker and lover of peace.

> Did not the Son of God come to earth to reconcile the world to the Father, to join people by indissoluble bonds of charity, and to make humanity his friend? He was an ambassador for me. He did my business. Solomon prefigured Him. Regardless of David's greatness, because he was a warrior defiled with blood, he was not permitted to

build the House of God. He did not deserve to be a figure
of the peaceable Christ.

Consider, O soldiers, if wars undertaken on the command of God profane, what is the result of wars undertaken for ambition or anger? If pagan blood pollutes the
meek king, what does Christian blood do? I pray the true
Christian prince to behold the image of his chief Prince.[2]

Erasmus quotes Jesus on his gift of peace as he takes leave
of his friends, his prayer for union among them "as We are
one," and the badge of mutual charity — not a soldier's uni-
form — that should mark his followers. Referring to the prayer
Jesus taught, the writer asks: "With what audacity do you call
upon the common Father while thrusting your sword into your
brother's vitals . . . It would be amazing for one branch of
a vine to fight with another. Is it not a more monstrous thing
for a Christian to fight with a Christian?"[3]

Erasmus has the whole teaching of Jesus on peace: the pro-
hibitions against competing for position, riches, and glory and
against the desire for vengeance; the command not to resist
evil; and the command to do good even to those who have
not deserved it.

When he likens Himself to a hen gathering her chickens
under her wings, how apt a symbol he uses to depict con-
cord. He is a gatherer. Is it proper that we Christians
should act like hawks? He is called the cornerstone.
Is it right that His vicars should move the world to
battle? . . . He reconciled Pilate and Herod, yet He cannot
bring His followers to agreement. . . .[4]

To one who knows the gospel, the arguments are irre-
futable and have a terribly modern ring: "It has come to the
point where it is considered folly to express yourself against
war or to praise what Christ himself praised."[5] We repeat, the
Turkish threat of that time was fully comparable to the Soviet
threat of ours. That made the demands of Erasmus all the more
courageous. But our point for the moment is the skill with

which he drew on the gospels to paint a portrait of Jesus under one important aspect.

In his lifetime effort to make the gospel a vital factor in the lives of his contemporaries, he wrote a long sermon in 1524 *On the Immense Mercy of God*. At one point he attacks his theme as follows:

> God will bestow mercy on someone even if another person asks for that mercy. The Canaanite woman wept, and her daughter was healed; the centurion had faith, and his servant was cured; the ruler of the synagogue begged, and his daughter was brought back to life. . . .
>
> If you dare not accost Jesus, if you cannot touch Him, at least stealthily touch the hem of His garment. Go to some godly person who can pray for you and commend you to the Lord. He often reveals His virtue in this way, for He is always ready to forgive.[6]

Paradoxically, Erasmus's great popular success written for the educated classes that could read Latin, *The Handbook of the Militant Christian* (1503), is not marked by the same evangelical sap as the treatises cited above. Here is an example of the skill Erasmus exercises in summoning the spirit of Jesus rather than the letter of the gospels:

> It is always a source of amazement to me that popes and bishops so indiscreetly wish to be called lords and masters when Christ forbade his disciples to be called either. We must ever bear in mind that there is but one Lord and Master, Christ Jesus our Head. The expressions apostle, shepherd, bishop are terms denoting office or service, not dominion or rule. Pope, abbot are terms meaning love, not power. Yet we are living in a world that has grown alien to the world of Christ both in doctrine and practice.[7]

Erasmus's valedictory was a discourse *On Minding the Peace of the Church* (1533). Seeing the church divided all around him, he deplored the divisions, while continuing his criticism of the endless desires for new wives and benefices and miters that brought no peace. His conclusion brought little comfort to the Reformers: "Therefore if we seek true peace of soul, let us persevere in the tabernacle of the Lord of Hosts, let us remain in union with the Catholic Church, which is Jerusalem and is built as a city."[8] Erasmus's formula for peace in Zion, that same church, was this:

> Let us enter [your tabernacle] without the stain of heresy and, advancing in faith, with works of love, practice justice, not of the law but of the Gospel, attributing to God all that we seem to do rightly. . . . Let us harken to the voice of the Lord, inviting us to true peace of soul: "Come to Me, all you who labor. . . . Take my yoke upon you and learn of me . . . and you will find rest for your souls."[9]

Drawing Strength from Jesus' Sufferings

Erasmus's great friend and fellow humanist was the layman, Thomas More, whose name Erasmus punned on in his *Encomium Moriae* ("The Praise of Folly"). The Dutchman wrote the satire while staying at More's home in 1509 and dedicated it thus: "First of all, there was your family name of More, which is as close to the Greek word for folly as you are far from the meaning of the word. Then, too, I suspected that you would approve this exercise of wit because you usually enjoy learned jokes of this kind which, at the same time, are not dull."[10] More went to meet the headsman's ax a quarter century later (1535) with a "mock" on his lips about needing a hand on the way up the scaffold but, when it came to coming down, shifting for himself. Unlike Erasmus, he was neither a preacher nor teacher so he gave his witness to the folly of the cross more in deed than in word.

More did, however, while spending his final days as a prisoner in the Tower of London in late summer of 1534, compose a *Dialogue of Comfort Against Tribulation*. It was his only substantial work not written in Latin, aside from an unfinished English version of *The History of King Richard III*. More had an extreme horror of physical pain. He was also a late medieval man, which means that his piety was centered on the passion of Jesus. In other writings he shows a doctrinal orthodoxy, even rigidity. Here he is warm and compassionate:

> Finally, cousin, to finish this piece with, our Saviour was Himself take[n] prisoner for our sake. And prisoner was He carried, and prisoner was He kept. . . . The time of His imprisonment, I grant well, was not long; but as for hard handling which our hearts most abhor, He had as much in that short while as many men among them all in much longer time. . . .[11]
>
> [Consider] the many sore bloody strokes that the cruel tormentors with rods and whips gave Him . . . the scornful crown of sharp thorns . . . His lovely limbs drawn and stretched out upon the cross. . . . the great long nails cruelly driven with hammers. . . . If we would, I say, remember these things . . . I verily suppose that the consideration of His incomparable kindness could not fail in such wise to inflame our key-cold hearts and set them on fire in his love.[12]

One finds reflections on the sufferings and death of Jesus everywhere in late medieval and Renaissance piety. It should not be the chauvinism of English-speakers that makes us say that, like Dame Julian two centuries before, More says it better than the rest. There is more to him. He was not writing to edify but to gain strength from Christ's passion for the "hard handling which our hearts most abhor."

Jesus as Savior by His Death on the Cross

Coming to the second Augustinian canon, Luther — whom the first, Erasmus, would not join in his break with the Roman Church — we come upon a medieval whose Jesus piety is chiefly a soteriology of the cross. Jesus died *propter nos*, for our sakes. The creedal phrase *pro nobis et propter nostram salutem*,

for us and for our salvation, is of greatest interest to Luther.
He writes in his *Preface to the New Testament* (1522):

> To know [Christ's] works and his life story is not the same
> thing as to know the gospel, because it does not mean
> that you know that He conquered sin, death, and the
> devil. Similarly, it is not knowledge of the gospel if you
> just know doctrines and rules of this kind. But you will
> know the gospel when you hear the voice which tells you
> that Christ Himself is yours, together with his life, teach-
> ing, work, death, resurrection, and everything that He
> has, or can do.[13]

Luther says in the same preface that if he had to dispense with
either the works or the preaching of Christ he would rather
do without the works than the preaching. "For the works are
of no avail to me, whereas His words give life, as He himself
declared."[14]

You will not, therefore, find the gospel picture of Jesus
enlarged or even much presented in Luther. It is as if he fears
that any such practice might make us forget "the gospel" —
namely, that it is by Christ's "work, His passion and death,
that He makes us righteous, and gives us life and salvation.[15]
Luther prefers John's gospel above the synoptics because it provides more of Jesus' words than the other three. His reason
for preferring Paul's epistles (and even Peter's) to Matthew,
Mark, and Luke is probably given in his commentary on Galatians: "The popish sophisters do [de]spoil us of this knowledge
of Christ and most heavenly comfort (namely, that Christ was
made a curse for us, that he might deliver us from the curse
of the law), when they separate him from sin and sinners, and
only set him out unto us as an example to be followed."[16]
Presenting Jesus as he was portrayed in the gospels could divert
believers from concentrating on his saving work. One wonders
if this was Saint Paul's reason for never presenting Jesus but
only the crucified and glorified Christ.

Martin Luther wished to take Jesus Christ out of people's
lives under one aspect so that he could restore him under

another — as he thought, a sounder and better one. Jesus had been portrayed for centuries as without sin because he was the Son of God born of the Virgin Mary. Yet Saint Paul wrote: God "made him who knew not sin to be made sin for us" (2 Cor. 5:21), and so he became, said Luther, "the greatest transgressor, murderer, adulterer, thief, rebel, blasphemer, etc. that ever was or could be in all the world."[17] Jesus is thus no longer an innocent person and without sins, having been made a sacrifice for the sins of the whole world.

This emphasis on Jesus as savior through his death on the cross meant that the Reformers came to absorb christology into soteriology. Convinced that meditation on Jesus' deeds or words could easily degenerate into a "work" of solely human origin, they proposed reflection on the divine deed only as shown forth on Calvary. The culmination of this attempt came in our time with Rudolf Bultmann's insistence that most of the material on Jesus in the first three gospels was, from a Christian viewpoint, expendable. For Bultmann it belongs back in the old eon, the period of the Law, because it does not proclaim Christ crucified and risen.

One finds Jesus quoted often in Luther's writings. There is the exhortation on many pages to read the Bible. Yet close examination shows that Jesus is not allowed to speak for himself so much as he is put in the service of a doctrinal conviction. That conviction is that "the gospel" is salvation by grace through faith. The medieval use of the Bible to which Luther was accustomed — namely, the employment of texts to bolster theological arguments — continued uninterrupted in his writings. He used the texts of his choice, chiefly the epistles of Saint Paul to the Romans and the Galatians, powerfully and with effect. But it has to be observed that the Erasmus whom Luther despised made the gospel picture of Jesus available to Christians better than he. Luther would doubtless acknowledge this and proceed with a snort to prove why "better" was worse. ("I hate Erasmus vehemently and from the heart," he wrote.[18] "I cannot endure his catechism [Erasmus's

Dilucida et pia expositio . . . , 1533] in which nothing is taught for certain; he confuses everything and calls it into doubt. . . .")[19] Luther was an apostle of certitude.

A Dogmatic Christ

John Calvin (1509-64), a lawyer's son and himself a lawyer, came from the provincial French town of Noyon. He was initially interested in classical studies but experienced a conversion at twenty-three while writing a commentary on the Psalms, which led him into divinity studies. If Luther was primarily a preacher, Calvin was primarily a theologian. His teaching on the two natures in Christ derives directly from the councils and the fathers whom he knew well, although he quotes the fathers only sparingly in his *Institutes of the Christian Religion* (final version 1559) and the councils almost never. Rather, he puts Scripture to use abundantly in the spirit of the fathers and the councils. His Jesus is a dogmatic Christ. He writes, in a passage that is typical of many:

> It was highly necessary . . . that he who was to be our Redeemer should be truly both God and man. It was his office to swallow up death; who could do this but he who was life itself? It was his to overcome sin; who could accomplish this, but righteousness itself? It was his to put to flight the powers of the world and of the air; who could do this, but a power superior to the world and the air? Now who possesses life or righteousness, or the empire and power of heaven, but God alone? Therefore the most merciful God, when determined on our redemption, became himself our Redeemer in the person of his only begotten Son!. . . . Clothed in our flesh, he vanquished sin and death, in order that the victim and triumph might be ours. . . .[20]

Warmer than this Calvin will not get, any more than Aquinas does in his *Summa Theologiae*. A difference is that we have a different Thomas on Jesus in the hymns and prayers attributed to him, art forms that do not survive from the equally fervent Calvin.

Reflecting on
What God Has Done for Us in Jesus

The *Catechismus* drawn up in 1566 by a team of Dominican friars by order of the Council of Trent was an adult handbook for preachers. Of its nature it is a nonpoetic exposition of the Apostles' Creed, the sacraments, the commandments, and prayer. Yet it does attempt to motivate priests to preach the Christian mysteries in an affective way. In the section on the third article of the creed, the "Roman Catechism," as it came to be called, says:

> Let the faithful see how Christ in his birth establishes us in salutary teaching before he begins to utter a syllable. He is born in need, born like an itinerant in a rough shed, born in a crude feeding-trough, born in the middle of winter; for thus does St. Luke write: *d) And while they were there the time came for her to be delivered . . .* (Luke 2:6-7). Could the evangelist have encompassed the total majesty of heaven and earth in simpler speech? He does not write that there was no room in the lodging place but no room for him who says: *e) The world and all that is in it is mine* (Ps. 49:12, Vulgate). Another evangelist gives similar witness: *f) Unto his own possessions he came yet his people received him not.* When believers have these matters before their eyes, let them consider that God wished to undergo the lowliness and fragility of our flesh in order to place the human race in the highest rank of dignity.[21]

If Calvin was the leading theologian of the age among the Reformers, the corresponding Catholics were the lesser figures Tommaso de Vio, OP, later Cardinal Cajetan (d. 1534), Melchior Cano, OP (d. 1560), and the abrasive Diego Laynez, SJ (d. 1565), the chief architect of Trent's theology. But the one

who put his stamp on the times from the Catholic side was
Saint Ignatius (born Iñigo) of Loyola (d. 1556). His *Ejercicios
Spirituales,* completed in 1535, were an invitation to a month-
long consideration of all that God had done for Christians in
Jesus Christ. The exercises were to be engaged in only once
in life, in the hope that a lasting conversion to Christ would
be achieved.

Ignatius's chief contribution to Western piety was his pro-
posal for a means to meditate on the "mysteries of the life of
our Lord." Calling on the use of all five senses, he prescribed
placing oneself (in one's imagination) in a gospel setting, seeing
the persons of the gospel narrative, entering into their feelings,
and ministering to their needs as if one were present there.
Some examples of his best known but by no means only technique of contemplation follow:

> Recall to mind the grievousness and malice of sin against
> our Creator and Lord. Let the understanding consider
> how in sinning and acting against Infinite Goodness, one
> has justly been condemned forever. Close with acts of
> the will, as mentioned above.
>
> *Colloquy.* Imagine Christ our Lord before you,
> hanging upon the cross. Speak with Him of how, being
> the Creator He then became man, and how, possessing
> life, He submitted to temporal death to die for our sins.
>
> Then I shall meditate upon myself and ask "What
> have I done for Christ? What am I now doing for Christ?
> What ought I do for Christ?" As I see him in this condi-
> tion, hanging upon the cross, I shall meditate on the
> thoughts that come to my mind.
>
> The colloquy is made properly by speaking as one
> friend speaks to another, or as a servant speaks to his
> master, now asking some favor, now accusing oneself for
> some wrong deed, or again, making known his affairs
> to Him and seeking His advice concerning them. Con-
> clude with the "Our Father."[22]
>
> *The second prelude* is to form a mental image of the
> scene and see in my imagination the road from Nazareth
> to Bethlehem. I will consider its length and breadth, and

whether it is level or winding through valleys and over
hills. . . .

    The first point is to see the persons: our Lady and
St. Joseph, the servant girl [!], and the child Jesus after
his birth. . . .[23]

    The third mode of humility is the most perfect. This
exists when . . . I desire and choose poverty with Christ
poor rather than riches, in order to be more like Christ
our Lord, when I choose reproaches with Christ thus suffering rather than honor, and when I am willing to be
considered worthless and a fool for Christ Who suffered
such treatment before me, rather than be esteemed as wise
and prudent in this world.[24]

The Basque ex-soldier led legions in this and other modes
of prayer. He must be named in conjunction with Francis of
Assisi as the one who gave modern Catholic Jesus piety its
shape. Introspective as he was, he understood the psychology
of the age's search for salvation. There is no mention of Saint
Paul in Ignatius's exercises, which means that the soteriology
the Reformers featured he did not. There is no mention of the
Holy Spirit. Ignatius is committed strongly to the force of grace
in human life, under the influence of which human effort oper-
ates. His prevailing sentiment, perhaps, is gratitude to the "Great
King" who has done so much for his subjects. They, in turn,
should do great things for him. The contrast between the Reformers' de-emphasis on the human capacity to respond and the
counter-Reformers' emphasis on the same could not be clearer
than in this saint of "election" and "discernment of spirits."

Jesus as Friend and Lover

One other great movement came out of late Renaissance Spain
besides that of the *Compañia de Jesus* (as Loyola called the
international band he formed in Paris, then brought to Rome).
It was the reformed branch of Carmelite friars and sisters, an
achievement of the hardy Teresa of Avila (d. 1582). Hers was
a warm embrace of the person of Jesus in her many writings,

all done at the behest of spiritual directors. She wrote extensively of her spiritual experiences in her states of prayer. While she reflected on them with remarkable psychological insight, she always remained eminently practical.

Her disciple and friend, Fray Juan de la Cruz, on the other hand, followed a strain of Platonic thought available through his Augustinian heritage that was more overtly mystical than Teresa's explorations. He knows the gospels well but prefers to hymn the love that Jesus bares his soul in, in terms of the Canticle, indeed of the traditional love songs of Spain, which he modifies and puts to Christian use. Here are a couple of indications of the heritage Saint Teresa left her sisters and brothers:

> It may be that our temperament, or some indisposition, will not allow us to think of the Passion, because of its painfulness; but what can prevent us from being with Him in His Resurrection Body, since we have Him so near us in the Sacrament, where He is already glorified? [Many a theologian of the last four centuries has not had the Eucharist as straight as this. Auth.] Here we shall not see Him wearied or broken in body, streaming with blood, exhausted by journeying, persecuted by those to whom He was doing such good, disbelieved by the Apostles. . . . Here we can behold Him free from pain, full of glory, strengthening some, encouraging others, before He ascends to the heavens. In the Most Holy Sacrament He is our Companion and it would seem impossible for Him to leave us for a moment. . . . With so good a Friend, so good a Captain at our side, Who came forward first of all to suffer, one can bear anything. He helps us; He gives us stength; He never fails; He is a true Friend!
>
> One day, when I was at prayer, the Lord was pleased to reveal to me nothing but His hands, the beauty of which was so great as to be indescribable. . . . A few days later I also saw the Divine face, which seemed to leave me completely absorbed. I could not see why the Lord revealed Himself gradually like this since He was later

to grant me the favour of seeing Him wholly, until at
length I realized that His Majesty was leading me according to my natural weakness. . . . Although this vision
[on Saint Paul's Day, of a complete representation of the
most sacred Humanity] was imaginary, I never saw it,
or any other vision with the eyes of the body, but only
with the eyes of the soul.[25]

A lyrical outburst seems the proper way to conclude a
selection of images of Jesus from this tortured century, so
familiar with depths and heights. It is Saint John of the Cross's
Madrigal "of Christ and the soul":

Once a young shepherd went off to despond:
how could he dance again? how could he sing?
All of his thoughts to his shepherdess cling,
with love in his heart like a ruinous wound.

The root of his sorrow? No, never the wound:
the lad was a lover and welcomed the dart
that lodged where it drank the red race of his heart —
but spurned by his fairest, went off to despond.

For only to think he was spurned, and by one
radiant shepherdess, drove him afar;
cost him a drubbing in foreigners' war,
with love in his heart like a ruinous wound.

The shepherd boy murmured: O murrain descend
on the traitor estranging my angel and me!
charming her vision that stares stonily
on the love in my heart like a ruinous wound.

Time passed: on a season he sprang from the ground,
swarmed a tall tree and arms balancing wide
beautifully grappled the tree till he died
of the love in his heart like a ruinous wound.[26]

7

The Move
into Modernity

It is probably deceptive to
present images of Jesus from classical Western sources, as we
have been doing in this series, because most people — beginning
with the Christian East — derived their view of him from quite
other sources. For one thing, this positive approach can lead
to the wrong conclusion that there was universal knowledge
of the Jesus Christ of faith abroad — whereas, in fact, there
was at the same time immense ignorance of him. The people
sang the Gloria and the Creed without knowing Latin, hence
without comprehension of the great conciliar affirmations and
acclamations these chants contained. They had the full biblical
narrative in the stained-glass windows of the twelfth- and
thirteenth-century cathedrals. Usually, however, these artful
renderings were placed so high on the walls and clerestory (so-
called because it "stood clear") that the details could not be
seen. It is romantic to lump all this magnificent art together as

"the Bible of the poor," for often its visual inaccessibility made it just as unavailable to the masses as their illiteracy did the carefully copied manuscripts of the Bible.

It was popular preaching that accomplished such exposition of the gospels as Europe knew — and there was not much of it until the advent of the friars. The reredoses that rose above altars ("rear," from *retro dorsum*) and the tympanums above church doors told biblical stories in wood and stone; but these were frequently scenes of the Last Judgment, extrapolated from the harsh endings to Matthew's parables and depicted in the manner of Dante's *Inferno*.

Some of the favorite gospel stories about Jesus were told and retold. Often Jesus' parables took on the same reality as the events of his life that were recounted by the evangelists. In this transmittal, the medievals were better interpreters than they realized. Much-loved were the infancy accounts of Matthew and Luke and the passion and risen life scenes of the four gospels. All were presented kaleidoscopically, with little account taken of the peculiar force of the telling — the context altering the text — in the work of this evangelist or that. Jesus' tempting in the desert was a popular favorite; likewise, any tale that described the putting to flight of demons. The miracles of healing and power were endlessly repeated, usually as if the first three evangelists had a full-blown Johannine christology of the Word of God in the flesh. The crowds reveled to hear of Lazarus, the poor beggar, vindicated while the rich man moaned for a drop of water on his tongue; of the woman taken in adultery — invariably supposed to be Mary Magdalene — who was told to go and sin no more and was appeared to first in the garden; of the wastrel son and the woman at the well and Simon Peter rescued from a drowning and Judas hanged.

These stories were very well known. So, too, was the legend of Christopher who bore the divine child across the stream, as well as the flowering rod of Joseph and the young Mary deposited at the temple to be reared by the priests.

Martin's cloak and the three kings' casks and the bones of Becket were somehow fused in the popular mind. It comprised the one story of a compassionate God and an all-forgiving Son, who needed the intervention of a Virgin Mother and the heavenly court to mitigate the rigors of God's stern judgment. The Holy Spirit was a dove and a flame of fire but not a divine presence integrated into everyday life. Jesus was Emmanuel, God with us. Father and Son were somewhere in the wings, not on center stage. The Lord Christ could do for them well enough as the fullness of deity.

That is why speaking exclusively about the writings of the theologians and mystics in a world of wayside shrines and feast days and patron saints for every ill and trade could give a false impression. The Jesus of many centuries was neither the Christ of the Christian Scriptures, nor of the creeds and councils, nor of two or three of these in combination. Still, the stable monks and nuns and the itinerant friars were vastly influential on the piety of the people, and they tended to have Jesus straight. The Reformers, who basically came out of Renaissance learning and city-based commerce — although they would have hotly denied this — likewise had their tens of thousands of followers among the masses; indeed, especially when abetted by friendly princes in whose territory the new religion was imposed. (*Cuius regio, eius religio.*) Even the visionaries of those ages lived to see their private gifts and revelations become a public treasure. Woven into this tapestry of wild and drab colors, rich and meager threads, was the face of Jesus: universal Savior, compassionate Healer, severe Judge, Son of God in human flesh.

An important change came with the reintroduction of Pauline thought into preaching by the "new men." This made of Jesus once again the one mediator with God in the work of salvation. The pantheon of saints was driven to flight, rendering the imaginative life of Christians poorer but restoring Jesus to the place he had never entirely lost in the concluding doxology of the canon: "Through whom and with whom and in whom all glory and honor are yours, almighty Father" and, from the conclusion of the three prayers of each Sunday and feast: "in the unity of the Holy Spirit, God." Through the revival of Pauline thought, the ancient trinitarian mode of prayer was being restored to a Europe that had never completely lost sight of it.

Different Images to Meet Different Needs

Central to this process of development was the truth that the various descriptions of Jesus reflected the spirit of the age in which each of the writers lived as much as they captured the reality of his person. To the poor populations of Egypt and rural Syria in the fifth century, Jesus' divinity drowned his humanity "like the ocean engulfing a drop of honey" because these powerless peoples felt no need of a powerless Christ. The people of medieval Europe could abide him as a helpless babe and the victim of cruel tormentors because their own sufferings helped them empathize with his. A literate Renaissance population gaining a sense of history insisted that only what was contained in the books of the apostolic age could describe Jesus accurately. Saint Paul, in providing a theory to account for human deliverance from sin — a theory that this anxious age needed as badly, even if it misconceived it — set large segments of Europe at ease. The burden of salvation was put exclusively on God's shoulders, where the times were convinced it belonged. Describing later times than those we have reached in our survey, *A New Catechism* (commissioned by the bishops of the Netherlands in 1966) says:

> We can now see very clearly, as we survey the efforts formerly [1800 to 1920] made to analyse the "life of Jesus," that the enthralling psychological descriptions mirrored not so much the mentality of Jesus as the spirit of the age in which each of the writers lived. During the Enlightenment, Jesus was seen as a teacher of great insight who spoke of God and virtue. In the age of Romanticism

he appeared as a "religious genius." Where Kantianism was influential he became an ethical teacher similar to Kant. In times of social upheaval, he was seen as a champion of social reform. And so on.[1]

This is a truism but an important one. Each era creates an image of Jesus to meet its needs.

In our last chapter we reached the sixteenth century in the West. It was a time when Catholics and Protestants differed over the nature of the church and the means of salvation, but remained largely at one over the person of Jesus Christ. For both, he was the perfect expression of the compassion of God. Complete trust in God through Jesus' intercessory power was the key to a salvation ardently longed for, regardless of where people stood on the Bible, the sacraments, or intercessors other than Jesus on earth or in heaven. There was a different conviction in the two camps over which was primary, God's sovereign will or the divine all-knowing intellect. The Reformers were Augustinian in the manner of Scotus, Ockham, and Biel; they were Platonist in outlook whether consciously or not. The Catholics were Thomist rather than Scotist in the mode of their adherence to Augustine, hence Aristotelian in outlook, but also largely affective rather than analytic through the influence of giants like Francis and Bonaventure, Loyola, and Teresa.

Saint Teresa of Jesus
and the Renaissance Spirit

We closed last time with a consideration of Loyola and Teresa, observing that their christology retained strong elements of exemplarity of the words and deeds of Jesus, whereas Luther and Calvin tended to confine themselves to grace-inspired faith in the deed of the cross. It is to Teresa of Jesus (1515-82) that we should like to return briefly for consideration of the Renaissance outlook before we contemplate the modern spirit, here defined as those ways of thinking and acting that bore the seeds of our own era.

Teresa records that early in her convent life she used to try to think of Jesus Christ, whom she called "our Good and our Lord," as present within her. If she thought about any incident in his life she would try to imagine it inwardly, but she confessed that her imagination was so poor that in those days she never succeeded in recreating Jesus' humanity.[2] This handicap would have made her a poor disciple of her younger countryman, Iñigo of Loyola. For years, Teresa writes, she prayed with the aid of books because her gift of understanding was weak and that of imagination weaker. When at a later date she grew more adept at placing all her confidence in God she acquired some skill in "making pictures of Christ inwardly." For many years before retiring at night, she wrote, she created in imagination the scene of Jesus praying in the garden.

> I used to think I felt better when I dwelt on those parts of His life when He was most often alone. It seemed to me that His being alone and afflicted, like a person in need, made it possible for me to approach him. . . . I was particularly attached to the prayer in the Garden, where I would go to keep Him company. I would think of the sweat and of the affliction He endured there. I wished I could have wiped that grievous sweat from His face, but I remember that I never dared to resolve to do so, for the gravity of my sins stood in the way.[3]

Yet, in the immediate context of these remarks, the saint repeats her constitutional incapacity to imagine: "Of Christ as Man I could only think: however much I read about His beauty and however often I looked at pictures of Him, I could never form any pictures of Him myself. I was like a person who is blind, or in the dark."[4] On the occasions when the darkness was pierced by a fleeting consciousness of the presence of God, this was induced by reflection on "His Passion, with its grievous pains, and on His life, which was so full of afflictions."[5]

Jesus' great love for humanity received most of Teresa's attention, and in contemplating it she received encouragement and joy. But of the contemplation of Jesus' joy or even of his

specific words she at first tells us little, except through passing references to Jesus' resurrection as the cause of a "virtuous
joy" in us. This great woman was a child of her time, and the
sixteenth century was an age of dread on the Catholic as on
the Protestant side. To pious believers, joy too often meant
the exuberant paganism of the Renaissance princes who re-
created in their imaginations the golden age of Athens or the
freedoms of Olympus. Teresa knew that comfort and benefit
were available to the tenderhearted, who grew exhausted in
thinking about the passion, from considering the power and
greatness of God in creatures.[6] But meditation on a scene like
Jesus' binding to the Pillar was the safest road until "the Lord
leads us to other methods."

Once she permitted herself a reference to Mark 3:21, with
the outburst to her confessor Ibañez: "Let us all be mad, for
the love of Him who was called mad for our sakes."[7] She writes
of numerous raptures and visions, during some of which her
nuns were required to hold her down as if she were in seizure.
She experienced appearances of Christ and our Lady and the
dead Franciscan confessor who had guided her, Pedro de
Alcántara. In describing these she was at pains to distinguish
them from the sight and sound of sense, simply "knowing"
that the persons were there and the words in which they
addressed her.

Chapter 22 of the Life contains an account of her esteem
for the humanity of Jesus, in opposition to those authors who
"advise us earnestly to put aside all corporeal imagination and
approach the contemplation of the Divinity.[8] She is not sym-
pathetic to their argument that even Christ's humanity can
impede attaining to perfect contemplation, an entirely spiritual
work. At the same time, Teresa says she speaks only of her way
and is not out to refute learned and spiritual men who hold
otherwise. There was a time when she was given to the "prayer
of quiet," which tried to banish everything corporeal from the
mind. Then, however, through the help of one who cured her
of this error, she began to experience the companionship of

Jesus — something she had previously known only in trial and temptation — in "being with Him in His Resurrection Body, since we have Him so near us in the Sacrament, where He is already glorified." Teresa shared this theological insight with Aquinas and Calvin, both of whom taught correctly, against the prevailing spirit of their ages, that the eucharistic Christ was no longer suffering but a Lord in glory. "Here we can behold Him free from pain, full of glory, strengthening some, encouraging others."[9] Then she enunciates the principle she had discovered and hoped thenceforth to live by:

> I can see clearly . . . that it is God's will, if we are to please Him . . . that this should be done through his most sacred Humanity, in Whom, His Majesty said, He is well pleased. . . . I have seen clearly that it is by this door that we must enter if we wish His Sovereign Majesty to show us great secrets. . . . We must look at His life — that is our best pattern.[10]

The saint expresses impatience with our wanting to become angels while we are still on earth, calling it ridiculous. "As a rule, our thoughts must have something to lean upon, though sometimes the soul may . . . need no created thing to assist it in recollection." At seasons of dryness,

> We have a very good friend in Christ. We look at Him as a Man; we think of His moments of weakness and times of trial; and He becomes our Companion. Once we have made a habit of thinking of Him in this way, it becomes very easy to find Him at our side, though there will come times when it is impossible to do the one thing or the other.[11]

She reports a time when she was at prayer and Jesus revealed to her "nothing but His hands, the beauty of which was so great as to be indescribable."[12] A few days later she saw his face. She could not understand this gradual self-revelation until she realized that she was being led according to her natural weakness.

> A most especial bliss, then, will it be to us when we see
> the Humanity of Jesus Christ; for, if it is so even on
> earth . . . what will it be when the fruition of that joy
> is complete? Although this vision is imaginary, I never
> saw it, or any other vision, with the eyes of the body,
> but only with the eyes of the soul.[13]

In these intellectual visions, Christ almost invariably
showed himself to her in his resurrection body, which was also
the way in which she saw him in the eucharistic host. Only
occasionally did he show her his wounds and as he was on
the cross or sometimes in the garden, "to strengthen me when
I was in tribulation."[14] Always, however, even when he wore
the crown of thorns or was carrying the cross, Jesus appeared
to Teresa in his glorified flesh. Like all the great saints of even
the church's most self-lacerating periods, she knew that Jesus'
exile and ours ends in glory. In her autobiographical "Book
of the Foundations," one of her most interesting writings, Jesus
appears regularly and in a most familiar way in the role of
Teresa's major superior. The day-to-day practicality of this
treatise and shorter ones like her sixty-nine "Maxims for Her
Nuns" provides relief from the intensity of writings like *The
Interior Castle* and *The Way of Perfection.* One is tempted
to forgive her all her flights and raptures when one reads: "God
deliver me from people who are so spiritual that they want
to turn everything into perfect contemplation, come what
may."[15]

The sobriety of Teresa on the subject of Jesus comes clear
by comparison with what H. A. Reinhold called the "enamored
ragings" of Saint Maria Maddalena de' Pazzi (1566-1607),
exhorter to pope and cardinals:

> She ran through the convent as if crazed with love, and
> cried in a loud voice: "Love, love, love!" And since she
> could not endure this conflagration of love she said: "O
> Lord, no more love, no more love!" . . . And she said
> to the sisters that followed her: "You do not know, belov-
> ed sisters, that my Jesus is nothing but love, yes, mad with

love. . . . You are . . . lovely and joyous, you refresh
and solace, you nourish and unite. You are both pain and
slaking, toil and rest, life and death in one. Is there anything that is not within you? . . . O Love, you suffuse
and transfix, you rend and bind, you govern all things,
you are heaven and earth, fire and air, blood and water.
You are both God and man."[16]

The Protestant visionary Jakob Boehme, a shoemaker of
Goerlitz (1575-1624), was much quieter voiced in his nine
treatises written in the last four years of his life and collected
as *The Way to Christ*. His great devotion to our Lord was
summed up in the holy name JESUS, which he saw as the
morning star and the fiery brightness of divine love. Boehme's
spirituality resembled that of Eckhart and the later George Fox
of the Society of Friends in its discovery of the divine light
within the individual. He writes in a "Prayer for Monday
Noon":

O dear Lord Christ, help me that I might always consider
Your humility, lowliness, and temporal poverty, and do
not let my mind lift itself above the simple, poor and
needy, so that my soul is not broken away from them,
so that in their misery they do not weep over me and my
way to You is not hindered. Help my heart to lie in the
dust for the simple, and always acknowledge that I am
not more than they, that my position is Yours, and that
I am only Your servant in it."[17]

Many a Christian saint over the centuries had served and
struggled for the poor, but here we have the beginnings of
acknowledgment that there is something out of joint in a society
that knows the wide chasm between rich and poor. The percep-
tion is faint but it is an opening. Later, in the Sixth Treatise,
those persons are fulminated against who "torment the poor
and the wretched, sucking their very sweat from them, viewing them as something to trample so that they themselves may
be important. 'All these do it to Christ Himself, and they belong
to His stern judgment.' "[18]

Boehme waxes polemical against a misconception of the deed of Christ:

> All hypocrisy by which we say, "Christ has paid and made satisfaction for sin; he has died for our sins," is all false deception (an empty useless comfort) if we also do not die to our sins in Him and draw on His merit in new obedience and live in it.
>
> He who is antagonistic to and an enemy of sin has Christ's sufferings for comfort. . . . But the external hypocrisy, the externally accepted sonship, is false and useless.[19]

A "Devout Life" for Lay People

We come into a more modern way of thinking with the bishop of Geneva, François de Sales (1567-1622). Boehme was a layman who wrote for the laity. De Sales was a cleric who was the first post-Reformation Catholic to try to put himself in the shoes of those laypeople of the noble and educated classes who were in search of "a devout life." His motto was "Live, Jesus." Its initial letters *VJ (Vivat Jesus)* are inscribed in a handsome box hedge beneath a statue of Mary that thousands of motorists driving north on Interstate 95 near Childs, Maryland, see on a property of the Oblates of Saint Francis de Sales. Their puzzlement must be great as they see Mary's statue with these two letters on the lawn at her feet. Victory over Japan? No, but victory over sin and selfishness, death and destruction, by the Living One. It was for this that de Sales lived and struggled.

He was a Frenchman whose life from the age of thirty-five was spent as bishop of the triple see of Geneva-Lausanne-Annecy, a Catholic diaspora in a Reformed stronghold. There he won the respect if not the love of those who viewed anything related to Rome as somehow corrupt. His outgoing gentleness was the answer. In today's world we call it an ecumenical spirit. When he writes about Jesus he does so in a traditional way bordering on dullness until an insight out of everyday living or the world of nature illumines the scene. He may have been a Nabokov before his time, tramping the Swiss hillsides with a butterfly net, but he certainly was someone who ate and digested Pliny the Elder's *Natural History*. At first, one finds oneself smiling with a faint superiority at the way he puts flora and fauna to use in the service of the gospel. A grudging respect gradually replaces this feeling. The illustrations, whether good or bad as biology and zoology, prove to be remarkably apposite. The man also has a gift for anecdote not encountered in spiritual writing up to this point. Observe his praise of the excellence of the search for solitude:

> On Mount Calvary [our Savior] was like the pelican in the wilderness which revives her dead chicks with her own blood. At his Nativity in a desolate stable he was the owl in a ruined building, mourning and weeping for our offenses and sins. At his Ascension he was like the sparrow flying up to heaven, which is, as it were, the rooftop of the world.[20]

With John 16:21 in mind, he says that believers have within their souls Jesus Christ, the most precious child in the world, and until he is entirely brought forth and born it is impossible to avoid suffering from the labor.[21] Human sufferings are nothing compared with Jesus' in quantity or quality. He will protect us against calumny if we go forward in his service with confidence and sincerity. He will protect our reputation, but if he permits it to be taken away from us it will either be to give us a better one or to make us profit by the humiliation we are subjected to.[22] Poverty is to be met at one's own door and embraced as the dear friend of Jesus Christ, "for he was born, lived and died in poverty. Poverty was his nurse throughout his entire life."[23] In times of temptation one should run in spirit to the Holy Cross. The love with which Jesus suffered on it was for you, de Sales writes to Philothea, the recipient of his proposed exercises. "It is certain that on the tree of the Cross the Heart of Jesus our beloved beheld your heart and loved it."[24] Just as an expectant mother, he continues, prepares for a child, Jesus, fruitful and heavy with you, plans to bring you forth to salvation and make you his child. This bishop saint never misses a chance to improve the occasion. He is totally predictable but he is never smug. One gets the feeling with every line that, in total simplicity, he is practicing every piety, every self-denial, every word he preaches.

Saint Thérèse of Lisieux and Spiritual Desolation

Is this Saint Francis described above a modern man, one who incorporates Jesus into his life as one of us might? At some times yes, at other times no. Thérèse of Lisieux (1873-97) does not at first strike us as being any more our contemporary than he, despite her greater proximity in time. Her life story was written because she was instructed to record it by her sister Pauline when she was Thérèse's prioress. It is a period piece in its rhetoric and its piety, an off-putting document in every way until one begins to read the text behind the text.

This young woman is terribly keen, determined, and by nature self-willed. The trip to see the pope and ask him for early entrance into Carmel was an exercise in manipulation. Nothing escapes her mastery of the situation. Whenever she employs biblical texts her use of them indicates her total grasp of their meaning. She is, on balance, one who experienced the divine absence far more than the divine presence. If spiritual desolation is the spirit of this age she is surely its patron saint. This woman who wanted to be a priest would have been an ardent feminist in our day, railing in holy impatience against the injustices worked on women in society and church. She writes a testament to a coming of age in the Spirit; the poor little rich girl who has everything, asks to be despoiled of it, and whose prayer is answered.

Thérèse says that in youth she asked the Child Jesus to make her his plaything, but one suspects that at that point it was the other way around. "It is your arms, Jesus, which are the lift to carry me to heaven."[25] Then came the terms of his assistance: strains on the relations among her and her siblings in a very small house; humiliations in the depths of her soul, nothing outward; a total loss of the sense of a life to come as she lay dying. "Don't imagine that I'm overwhelmed with consolations. I'm not. My consolation is not to have any in this life. Jesus never manifests Himself nor lets me hear his voice."[26] But she never gives up on him. She knows that when he said at Jacob's well, "Give me to drink," he was thirsty for love. Her response is: "In the heart of the church, who is my Mother, I will be love."[27]

She prayed that her two sisters would not be sent to the Carmel in Saigon; it never happened. She herself longed to be assigned to Hanoi. Her *Story of a Soul* is a very modern book, not in its awareness of geography but in the anguish of its interpersonal relations. "But what I demand is love," she writes. "I care now about one thing only — to love You, my Jesus."[28]

8

The Modern Critics and Their Heirs

In the winter of 1899-1900 the Protestant historian of dogmas, Adolf von Harnack, delivered at the University of Berlin a series of lectures that came to have an immense influence. He entitled them "The Essence of Christianity." They were presented in English as *What Is Christianity?* shortly after their appearance in Germany.[1] Wilhelm Bousset faulted Harnack's performance at its publication for not giving sufficient importance to the background of contemporary thought in its account of the preaching of Jesus.[2] He was joined in this by Albert Schweitzer who criticized him colorfully for leaping "across a cleft . . . in an ice-floe," namely from gospel times to 1899, while ignoring "the contemporary limitations of Jesus' teaching."[3] The limitations Schweitzer was sure he had discovered came with the spelling out of the conviction of Johannes Weiss in a brief, 67-page essay that in Jesus' lifetime the final age was thought to be imminent.[4] Schweitzer understood this to have altered the course of all study of Jesus in the gospels. Harnack, meanwhile, was accused of supposing in his research into the early church that Christianity was a Hellenistic movement even in its Palestinian origins. This kept him from seeing or understanding "the eschatological character of the appearance of Jesus and his preaching of the imminent advent of the Kingdom of God."[5]

The discovery that Jesus was conditioned by his religious tradition and times was a matter not quite a century old by 1900. Whatever Harnack's historical limitations, he did what the Christian centuries had long been doing by leaping from the gospel period to his own age and finding in Jesus' person and teaching some One and some thing not bound by time and space in the ordinary sense. The gospel, he said, either came with its time and departed with it, or else contains something of permanent validity. Harnack, in fact, presented Jesus as a Protestant figure of the Enlightenment whose primary concern was ethical, indeed someone not terribly unlike himself. Still, the portrait of Jesus sketched in *What Is Christianity?* has its memorable features. The Berlin professor expresses the well-nigh universal interest in Jesus this way: "There is something touching in the anxiety which everyone shows to rediscover himself, together with his own point of view and his own circle of interest, in this Jesus Christ, or at least to get a share of him."[6]

Harnack thought that the Beatitudes contained Jesus' ethics and his religion "united at the root, and freed from all external and particularistic elements.[7] He might be surprised to learn how steeped the Matthean Beatitudes were in Jewish apocalyptic thought, but he would have made a quick recovery. Their kernel, we might expect him to say, was humility — the love of God of which we are capable — and the heart of Jesus' message was toward the good out of which everything that is good springs and grows. "The love of one's neighbor is the only practical proof on earth of that love of God which is strong in humility.[8] A little later he will hold that "Ultimately the kingdom is nothing but the treasure which the soul possesses in the eternal and merciful God."[9] The whole of the gospel, from which we must keep free any alien element, is "God and the soul, the soul and its God."[10] This concern with God as Father and Jesus as the means or way to him, but not more, is central to Harnack's thought.

Johannes Weiss's distinctive contribution was to disclose that Jesus' activity, as the first three gospels report it, was governed by a strong and unwavering feeling that the messianic time was imminent. The Kingdom of God was to be brought on by God. No human effort could establish it, not even that of Jesus. Weiss thought that Jesus' "messianic consciousness" consisted of the certainty that, when God had established the Kingdom, judgment and rule would be transferred to him: Jesus reigning under the higher sovereignty of God.[11] This is all told fairly straightforwardly in the gospels. Weiss's bombshell in the Protestant liberal camp was his maintaining that Jesus was completely convinced of the reality of his own apocalyptic thought world — and that he would not have been pleased to see himself presented as a lofty moralist who had no interest in "Jewish particularities."

But while Weiss was concerned to lay bare the terms of Jesus' actual proclamation of the Kingdom of God, he demanded that modern Christians admit that they use the term *kingdom* in a different sense from Jesus' use. Contemporaries do not, in fact, share the eschatological attitude that "the old order is passing away" (2 Cor. 5:17). The Protestants of Weiss's acquaintance tended to say that the Rule of God is the highest religious good and the supreme ethical ideal.[12] But that, he maintains, is to part company with Jesus at the most decisive point. Weiss proposes that the closest we can come to Jesus' message is to preach, instruct, and reflect that, while the world will further endure, we as individuals will soon leave it. "Thereby we will at least approximate Jesus' attitude. . . . We do not await a Kingdom of God which is to come down from heaven to earth and abolish this world, but we do hope to be gathered with the church of Jesus Christ into the heavenly *basileia* [kingdom; rule]. In this sense we, too, can feel and say, as did the Christians of old, 'Thy Kingdom come!'"[13]

Albert Schweitzer was sure of the correctness of Weiss's instinct that Jesus' Kingdom of God was supramundane and wholly future, an insight that only Reimarus among modern Europeans had had before him.[14] He deplored, however, the confinement of the idea by Weiss to Jesus' preaching. Eschatology was the assumption of every aspect of Jesus' life.[15] What, then, was to be made of this fact, which proved both thoroughgoing skepticism about eschatology and thoroughgoing eschatology (a dogmatic system that built upon acceptance of it) wrong? Two things, Schweitzer thought: the acknowledgment that Matthew was written before Mark, hence was historically more reliable because it attributed more material about the endtime to Jesus; second, the admission that "that which is eternal in the words of Jesus is due to the very fact that they are based on an eschatological world view, and contain the expression of a mind for which the contemporary world with its historical and social circumstances no longer had any existence."[16] The historical Jesus influenced individuals by the individual word, Schweitzer thought, not by a conception of his life as a whole that remained a mystery even for the disciples. Jesus is interpreted as the teacher of an ethic in a world-affirming spirit, but in fact he was the eschatological Son of Man, an authoritative ruler in a world-negating spirit.

Modern Catholic Eschatologies

Catholics who read this early twentieth-century history will tend to divide themselves according to age. The older ones, having missed the liberal Protestant reading of the gospels, will reflect that Weiss's proposed application of the eschatological preaching of Jesus to preparation for death is the only one they ever had shared with them from childhood. A "particular judgment" was fully expected, with a shadowy "general judgment" to follow — one which seemed somehow unnecessary, even though the catechism said that it was meant to proclaim publicly the shame of the wicked and the glory of the just.

But those exposed to the study of the gospels in high school or college from 1950 onward would have heard a good deal about Jewish end-expectation and likewise been told either of two things about it: apologetically, that Jesus could not have been wrong in what he thought about the last days and his role in them; and inaccurately, that Jesus, Paul, and the synoptic evangelists all lived in lively expectation of "the end of the world."

One fruit of the last century of study of the Christian Scriptures is, indeed, a heightened awareness of the Jewish apocalyptic outlook. This has been accompanied by a twofold literalism regarding it, the one aspect as unhelpful as the other. The first maintains that everything will come to pass just as described — a painful misconception of the nature of religious myth. The second — highly sophisticated — maintains that nothing in Jewish apocalypticism is to be understood literally except the time schedule. That was the one thing the Jews of Jesus' day believed which we should credit. Everything else was poetry; the proximity of "the end" was time and history. The reason this sole exception was made seems to be that the Christian Scriptures tell us of an early alteration of the myth by people who lived outside the myth. The evangelist John surely did this with his mentality that "the kingdom is now." Luke did the same by both living in hope of the end but recording in various ways that "my master is a long time in coming" (Luke 12:45), that is, that the delay of the *parousia* is a mystery his church is facing. The author of 2 Peter most clearly records calling apocalypticism in question when he tells of the mocking of those who ask: "Where is that promised coming of his? Our forefathers have been laid to rest, but everything stays just as it was when the world was created" (3:4). Already a gentile church has begun to live outside the Jewish myth. It has done so ever since and misconstrued it from a distance in a variety of ways all these years. Lately, but only lately, the church begins to be at ease with the thought world so foreign to it that Jesus inhabited.

Bultmann and the "Jesus of History"

We are touching here on an important modern problem. Because Jesus was a person in history and is viewed by believers in him as the Redeemer of the human race, the gospels have been taken as a historical record of him almost from the start. For a century or so now it has begun to come clear that, starting with Mark, they were a historicized eschatology. This has sent the learned on an earnest search for "the Jesus of history." There is no harm in this but great gain, provided that the Christian tradition is not forgotten — that the risen and glorified Christ, the same one as Jesus of Nazareth, is the only one proclaimed by the church. To assume that the reconstructed Jesus of pre-Easter days is the only Jesus we can proclaim honestly, given our modern historical knowledge, is to be untraditional in terms of religious faith.

Rudolf Bultmann did not solve the problem quite that way. He engaged in a remarkable research into the Jesus of history, trying to get behind the forms of proclamation that the gospels employed. Having published these laborious inquiries in *The History of the Synoptic Tradition*[17] and in *Jesus and the Word*,[18] he became convinced on theological grounds that only John and Paul proclaimed the risen Christ as the object of faith. This meant for him that the first three gospels were composed of pre-kerygma materials that belonged in the old eon preceding the one inaugurated on Easter Day. The church had for centuries lived at ease with the bipolarity of a message *of* Jesus and a message *about* Jesus by harmonizing the two — beginning with the canonizing process of the books of the Christian Scriptures. Bultmann thought that this highly inconsistent procedure ought to stop.

In *Jesus and the Word* a number of familiar Protestant prejudices of that time shine through. The book is anti-ascetical and anti-mystical; it discovers Jesus to have been anti-cult and anti-sacrament. Already the "existential" interpretation of the Christian Scriptures begins to appear in Bultmann's writings, making of Jesus one who calls us to decision so that authentic human selfhood may come of the choice. "Jesus sees man and his life . . . as absolutely insecure before what confronts him. A man cannot . . . in the moment of decision fall back upon principles, upon a general ethical theory which can relieve him of responsibility for the decision; rather, every moment of decision is essentially new."[19] Bultmann is helpful in pointing out what were editings by the church of Jesus' utterances, but the Jesus of history who remains — marvelous in his obedience to the will of God — comes through as something of an ideologue once Bultmann has stripped away his apocalypticism and molded him in his own image.

Other Influential Protestant Scholars

Bultmann's student, Günther Bornkamm, wrote what was probably the most satisfactory critical book in this vein, entitled *Jesus of Nazareth*.[20] It begins to show the shortcomings brought to light by thirty years of subsequent scholarship and is blind to the virtues of Judaism, like most theological work from Germany, but its special insights into the Jesus of the gospels are rich. Far less satisfactory is Hans Conzelmann's *Jesus*, a translation of a long encyclopedia article presented in book form.[21] C. H. Dodd's *The Founder of Christianity* is a series of lectures delivered in 1954 and prepared for publication fifteen years later.[22] The English Congregationalist scholar is less apodictic in tone than his continental confreres — also more conservative historically in the British manner. While his book is gracefully written, it begins to show its age. Thus, "Jesus at any rate allowed himself to be condemned to death for claiming to be (in Jewish terms) Messiah"[23]; [Mark was] less of an author and more of a compiler than the others. . . . he appears to have reproduced what came down to him with comparatively little attempt to write it up in his own way"[24] — two positions no longer held by the best scholars.

For our purposes it should be pointed out that the four books just dealt with are more dependable than not as history. Moreover, the author of each is at pains to proclaim the gospel that was Jesus, rather than merely act the part of the historian.

An interesting presentation in this line is Geza Vermes's *Jesus the Jew*, the work of a Hungarian scholar at Oxford who was for a period of his youth a Catholic and a priest. The research is mildly tendentious because of the author's desire to recreate a nonsupernatural Jesus and a Jewish Christianity of the late first century about which we have no hard evidence. Perhaps if we had *The Gospel of the Ebionites*, with a clear indication that it predated A.D. 100, Vermes might be sustained in his views. Lacking any such document, he is forced to theorize that the Greek-speaking church, which would include the four evangelists, completely misconstrued the true intention of Jesus. Vermes makes many valid points about the Judaism of gospel times, but his Jesus is not convincing because so much is denied of him that the evangelists affirmed.

Catholics Rediscovering Jesus' Humanness

Karl Adam, a Catholic at the state university of Tübingen, achieved a notable breakthrough with his *Christ Our Brother* published in four chapters in 1926 but more fully four years later.[25] A systematic theologian, Adam was abreast of the new critical learning but committed to the creeds and councils on Jesus in a way the critics were not. Early, lyrical chapters on "Jesus and Prayer" and "Jesus and Life" contain passages like the following (corrected from the German):

> Away then with Nietzsche's supposition that Jesus never laughed. How is it possible that He should not Himself have known a deep and pure joy, who was preaching the

pure gospel of the Father, and who in all joy and in all sorrow recognized God's infinite power and goodness? Jesus loved people and loved their life in the will of His Father. He was drawn to humanity not merely by its tears but by its laughter also.[26]

The full, broad stream of pure prayer which Jesus poured out to His Father was transformed into love of humanity, and came back to the poor and sick and sinful as redeeming and sanctifying power. Not that he was one of those simple enthusiasts who make a religion of the service of humanity; He had no interest in humanity as an end in itself, but in humanity as part and parcel of God's purpose; and regarding humanity as subject to God's will, He was able to give it a divine value.[27]

Much that Adam writes about Jesus in his early pages had been said by others as well. The true worth of his book to the Catholicity of the 1920s and 1930s comes when he traces historically the "one-sided prominence given to Christ's divinity and the obscuration of his humanity."[28] Relying on Herwegen and Jungmann, neither then available in English, he looks into the effect the Gnostic, Monophysite, and Pelagian struggles had on the church's image of Jesus Christ and its corporate liturgical prayer. "Gnostic piety and morality did not form a life lived in Christ and inspired by the Holy Spirit, but an individual and independent life. . . . Father Jungmann points out that the Arian heresy, in denying the Son's essential equality with the Father and full divinity, had a remarkable effect, by contrary reaction, on the Eastern liturgies generally. . . . St. Basil the Great and St. Athanasius [recast the ancient formulas so that] the ancient expression of Christ's mediatorial function, 'through the Son' was abandoned."[29] Adam stated starkly:

There is really now no longer any individual or isolated person, for we are all members of Christ and He is our Head. As there is one head, so there is but one body.

And that is the central point of the glad tidings of the gospel. The vital fact is not that God dwelt bodily

among us and that we can see the glory of God in the
face of Christ Jesus, but that this God is our brother, that
He is of one blood with us, that He is the Head of our
body. Of course the divinity is an essential element in
the picture of Christ. If Christ were not true God, then
the infinite gulf between God and the creature would not
be bridged in the person of Jesus. That was the point of
the fierce struggle with the Arians. . . . But this divine
element is not the only element in the picture of Jesus;
nor is it even the prominent element, during the time of
this world. Rather it is the golden background from which
His human activity stands out and from which it draws
its secret strength and redeeming power.[30]

This is the kind of thinking about Jesus that, in its return
to the church's oldest tradition, led to a generation of teachers
like Beauduin and Guardini, Mersch and Congar, Philips,
de Lubac, and Rahner — all of whom made Vatican II possible.
For Adam saw that a Jesus Christ dissociated from the church
of fellow humans that prayed in his name led to every sort
of individualism and sentimentalism. Veneration of the exclusively divine or exclusively human in him was the tragic
history of heresies. It is the challenge of the present century
to root them out and replace them with Catholic christological
faith in Jesus.

Karl Barth and "Neo-Orthodoxy"

In the Protestant world, something was coming to birth at Basel
in Switzerland after World War II that would put Jesus Christ
solidly in the center of consciousness. It was the dialectical
theology of Karl Barth (d. 1968), sometimes referred to as "neo-
orthodoxy." In lectures over many semesters at that city's
university faculty of theology, Barth presented what became
his never-to-be-completed *Church Dogmatics*. He so featured
the teaching of the Christian Scriptures that Jesus Christ is the
world's Redeemer that he has been accused of reshaping the

gospel as a Christ-centered *christology* rather than a traditional God-centered *theology*. Whatever the case, he certainly challenged any who would view Jesus as the mere teacher of a sublime ethic directed worshipfully toward God as Father. To read him is to hear the great christological councils and the church fathers come alive in proclaiming their functional (not their ontic) christology, i.e., what God *did* in Christ, not how God *was* in Christ. Barth writes in that classic work, with his customary vigor:

> The mystery of [Christ's] passion . . . is to be found in the person and mission of the One who suffered there and was crucified and died. His person: it is the eternal God Himself who has given Himself in His Son to be man, and as man to take upon Himself this human passion. His mission: it is the Judge who in this passion takes the place of those who ought to be judged, who in this passion allows himself to be judged in their place. . . . [God] gives himself to be the humanly acting and suffering person in this occurrence. He Himself is the subject who in his own freedom becomes in this event the object acting or acted upon in it.[31]
>
> And because this One is also man, every man in his time and place is changed, i.e., he is something other than what he would have been if this One has not been man too. It belongs to his human essence that Jesus too is man, and that in Him he has a human Neighbour, Companion and Brother. Hence he has no choice in the matter. . . . He cannot break free from this Neighbour. He is definitely our Neighbour. And we as [human beings] are those among whom Jesus is also a man, like us for all his unlikeness.[32]

Barth's ringing declarations present Christ as Savior in a way that is fairly easily identified as the work of an heir of John Calvin. Ernst Käsemann does something similar as a disciple of Martin Luther in his *Jesus Means Freedom*, an ironically witty book that makes of Jesus the same kind of excoriator of modern religiosity that he was in his own time.[33] It should not be missed for its valuable insights into the actual Jesus Christ of the Christian Scriptures.

Toward a Christology for Our Times

A spiritual heir of Saints Dominic and Thomas Aquinas, meanwhile, gives promise of writing a theology of Christian faith and life — one that will put the Jesus of the gospels, with his teaching and deeds of power, at the heart of the mystery of salvation. This is Edward Schillebeeckx, OP, whose lengthy studies, *Jesus: An Experiment in Christology*[34] and *Christ: The Experience of Jesus as Lord*,[35] are preliminary to a theology of redemption unlike that which had its tone set by Saint Paul in his stress on the cross and resurrection.

The Flemish Dominican indicates what he is preparing to do, not only in the mighty tomes themselves but in a prescriptive essay that points to the critical significance of the absence from the creeds of Jesus' public life.[36] It is a fundamental Christian conviction that in the coming of Jesus *God makes himself near to us* and it therefore *must*, in one way or another, find a place in the credo of our faith.[37] The conviction that the person of Jesus has, for believers, a significance for universal history means that a formal theology must incorporate that. Until now, expression of this conviction was left to the liturgical proclamation of the gospels and, since the invention of printing, Bible reading. The following passage is a fitting one with which to close these chapters, for it describes so aptly what Jesus means to the oppressed of Auschwitz and Treblinka, of Uganda and Guatemala.

> We must indeed remain fully aware that, as in the Yahwist tradition, Jesus does not so much introduce a new doctrine of God as cast a prophetic and particularly penetrating glance at the way in which the notion of God functioned concretely in the society of his times at the expense of the "little ones." Jesus unmasked a conception

of divinity that holds humanity in bondage. He fought for a vision of God as liberator of humanity, "Redemptor hominis" — a vision that has to be concretized in the conduct of life of each and all. That is why the names of God and Jesus become the bearers in the Gospels of a fruitful and liberating power. All religion that produces, in whatever fashion, dehumanizing fruits is either a false religion or a religion that has lost contact with itself, that no longer understands itself. This criterion of "humanization" proclaimed by Jesus, this passion for humanity's being human, for its healthy state, its identity and its integrity is by no means a reduction of religion, as the enemies of Jesus (then and now) fear. It is, on the contrary, the basic condition of its possibility and human credibility. Moreover, it is the only logical conclusion of the Christian vision of the God who is proclaimed as love.

It is of this God and no other, that Jesus is the "great symbol": *the image of the invisible God* (Col. 1:15; cf. 2 Cor. 4:3-4). At the same time, Jesus also put himself forward as the model of what the human being must be, the just, true, good way to be human."[38]

9

Some Contemporary Images of Jesus

Within the last forty years with the end of World War II — a watershed in the life of the globe — the figure of Jesus has had some remarkable adventures. Perhaps the most striking and significant of these is the way he has been viewed as a symbol both of the world's oppressed and of the liberation, by his teaching, of those thus oppressed. The first conception of his role is not new. In his victim status Jesus has long been turned to as God's open ear to the cry of the poor. With the rising consciousness of the downtrodden, their sense of victimization by the rich and the propertied grows. Many heed the promise of justice that Marxism holds out. Others respond to their lot in fierce anger and resentment. Jesus provides an alternative model, wherever he is encountered in the gospel lived at full strength.

The hymns of American slaves were perhaps the best modern articulation of the theme of Jesus as both sufferer and deliverer from suffering. The Africans adopted the religion of their Christian masters, in the first instance, because they had to: They later came to profess it out of wholehearted conviction. Christianity in theory, as they quickly perceived, did not permit the terrible injustices that were being heaped on them. More than that, its rhetoric of release from Egyptian slavery could be indulged in freely because the Christian slave-owners had spiritualized it to a point where it had no reality in the social order. If you were a slave, however, Moses and the Pharaoh and Mary's suffering boy-child had to be looked at differently. His resurrection after his ordeal — their ordeal — had made him "King Jesus." The paradox that came of this was that the Negro spirituals, as they were called, were composed as grimly serious outcries of protest, at the same time that biblical religion was being taken as a parable of sin and grace and not the protest against social evil it was meant to be. "Anybody talk about heab'n ain' goin' dere. Heab'n! Heab'n!" was beamed from the tar-paper chapel to heaven and to Massa's big house with an equal fervor.

Some armed revolutionaries in contemporary Latin America have claimed Jesus as their chief patron. As regards the New Testament record, they do not have a strong case. An English clergyman and academic, S.G.F. Brandon pressed the case as far as it would go. Students of the period and of the gospel texts, like Oscar Cullmann, have convinced the rest that it did not go very far. Jesus undoubtedly had freedom fighters among his close associates. How could he be a Galilean of the first century, zealous for the religion of the people of Israel, and not have them? But the gospel evidence yields a man of peace in Jesus, not a violent challenger of the social order. The image of Jesus as a Che Guevara before his time fails lamentably.

One that does not fail is Jesus as an oppressed and homeless person able to stand for the world's poor. The Lucan story of the circumstances of his birth contribute heavily to this image. The account of a newly married couple forced by a powerful colonial empire to temporary migrant status is one that millions can identify with. The other gospel phrase contributing to the picture of Jesus as a man of the dispossessed is the one that says that the foxes have holes and the birds nests but the Son of man has nowhere to lay his head. The gospels describe him as a village artisan, a person who unless he failed to work at his trade could expect a comfortable livelihood. He opted, however, for the life of an itinerant teacher. His charismatic calling led him to abandon the several obligations of a man of his culture, namely to inherit property, start a family, and witness the name carried on through the third and fourth generations.

His execution at the hands of the occupying power cut all this short. It was involuntary, save for the theological interpretation of willing acceptance the evangelists put on it. The operative fact, however, is that Jesus chose the counter-cultural existence that set him on a collision course with power. He is an authentic figure of powerlessness in the hands of forces beyond ordinary human control, a voice for the people which, once raised, has to be heeded or stilled. Whoever has heard of Jesus of Nazareth has heard of a just man who was an innocent sufferer. The fact that millions today are in that position, the victims of stupidity and greed and lust for power, makes him a rallying point for the exploited of the nations.

Added to this paradigmatic aspect of Jesus' career is the fact that Christian preaching has always viewed his being raised from the dead by a just God as a liberation from dark forces. These are chiefly sin and death. The first has long been viewed in Jewish history as the cause of the second. Jesus' coming forth from the tomb has been seen from earliest days as the fulfillment in type of his people's deliverance. The paschal mystery is traditionally preached as a theology of liberation.

There is nothing trendy about this. The modern problem is, which forces holding the human spirit captive can be identified unequivocally with the forces of sin and death? The ones that actually deal death to innocent hundreds of thousands, indeed millions, would seem to be the answer. The theological basis for a Jesus seen as the liberator of the oppressed is, in any case, the mystery of Easter.

Jesus is not a person universally hailed in the present age. Many angry women see in him someone manipulated by the churches to continue male domination over them. They have this much on their side: whenever the feminist struggle is mounted, in whatever hemisphere, the theological argument is made against it that God was teaching through the maleness of Jesus that things could not have been otherwise. From this it is quickly concluded that global patterns of male dominance have a certain divine sanction. The response of the women who care deeply about their involuntary subordination has been to stress the Christ or Word in Jesus as sexless, being an utterance of deity itself. The exchange that ensues is profoundly regrettable because a specious historical argument is countered with a flight from history. Not until the male principle of church leadership abandons its time-conditioned exclusiveness can women believers take it seriously as spiritual authority. Jesus by a twist of fate becomes the symbol of male oppression. He is held hostage, first by men and then in reaction by women. Whatever is brought to the fore about his astounding freedom from the sexist patterns of his age will be of little effect until male believers emulate him in it. He is rendered an inauthentic witness to God until he is freed from the bondage in which the church has put him.

The Father-Son imagery at the heart of Christian speech about God has outlived its usefulness in some quarters. A massive rehabilitation of the female as fully human is required. Language patterns are only the sign of what is needed. The reality is a churchwide acknowledgment in deed that a woman's capacity to reproduce and bear says nothing about her subordinate status. She can do all that a man can do and more. Women in the role of motherhood — which not all women in their freedom choose, or by circumstances may choose — are not to be idealized in order thereby to be victimized. Jesus, so long looked to by women as all that the men of their acquaintance are not, has been taken from them. They know exactly where he is laid: in a tomb of unavailability by male believers who use him as the symbol of their ascendancy. He must be restored to life. Only male Christians can do this, in response to a grace that up until now they are resisting.

The sin is by no means one of the clergy only. Sexist society is the offender and it is everywhere on the globe. "Oh, that is a North American problem, a problem of western Europe." The facile dismissal is nonsense. It is a problem wherever there are men and women trying to make a life together, especially where the supposition that Christian faith is true prevails. Women, who have always been Jesus' great lovers and friends, are being despoiled of him and men scarcely know that it is happening.

Jesus is at the same time being restored to millions in a variety of guises. One of the less attractive occurs in conservative evangelical circles where he is flourishing as an authority figure. He has become the *ipse* of a new *ipse dixit:* "Jesus said it and that is all there is to it."

An authority figure he surely is. The fourth gospel has given Christians the conviction that when they hear his voice they hear the voice of God. But even in that gospel and surely in the others he is a figure of mystery whose words must be long reflected on. They are to be thoughtfully questioned and above all lived before they will yield any meaning. Jesus as an oracle or answering machine who utters commands that require no explanation is someone the New Testament is unfamiliar with.

The early councils produced the faith-pronouncements about him that we need. He does not require being saddled with new dogmas, least of all one that teaches that no dialogue is needed once a saying of his from the gospels has been uttered. This oracular role puts Jesus in a perilous position. He becomes less than human, and divine only in the sense that he is a puppeteer who requires people to jump when the verbal string is pulled. The homage Christians pay to Jesus becomes other than good when it robs them of their freedom, programming them in a non-human way. Jesus is being put to such use all over the conservative Christian world.

The good news to offset this is that Jesus is being held in veneration by ever new populations. This is chiefly true among the young who see in him the fulfillment of all that goes unfulfilled in the adult world around them. There is a little manipulation of Jesus here but it is not predominant. It includes claims for his compassion to the point where there is no weakness or desire he will not condone. In such cases his boundless understanding is substituted for the demands of God he accepted and laid upon others.

By and large he is turned to as someone who will see into the human heart in a way the churches will not. The church never claimed anything other than this, but it sometimes forgets it in its attempts to be aligned with the Lord of its own imaging. Young people and young adults have a childhood remembrance of the church they last did business with. It is often so identified in their minds with parental control that they cannot distinguish the two. The result is that the Jesus of recent discovery or invention becomes the attractive opposite to all who claim identity with him in the church. Any such Christ-church claim is taken to be preposterous on the face of it. This hasty judgment leaves both the churches and young people the poorer.

Jesus is a countercultural figure, to be sure. Sometimes that culture is the life of the churches. But he looks for allies in the churches to go counter with him to the culture that John calls "the world." The impetuousness of youth and the incomprehension of age together rob Jesus of his best allies in the formation of young and vigorous churches. The local congregation or the larger communion that embodies Christ to the world should be living proof that he and it are not meant to be at odds, that there is no Christ in his fullness apart from the church.

This has been a book about Jesus Christs. He is one, but the prismatic refractions of him are many. Lover, warrior, patrician and plebeian of the spirit, God strong and immortal, son of peasant stock — he is all of these. He is many more things besides. The writer can only hope he has done something useful by assembling what a limited number of interpreters of Jesus have made of him.

The gospel of Mark ends at 16:8, an unfinished book. So does the Acts of the Apostles at 28:28. What are they saying to us? "Go and live the story out. Enrich the world by yet another incarnation of Jesus Christ within you." The Christian is under mandate to spread the word.

That means spreading the Word — in the persons of those of every culture and tongue and people under heaven.

Notes

Introduction

1. *First Catechetical Instruction*, 40.
2. *Sermon on the Lord's Passion*, 4.

Chapter One

1. Bruce Vawter, *This Man Jesus: An Essay Toward New Testament Christology* (New York: Doubleday, 1973). Also in paperback as an Image Book of the same publisher.
2. 1 Clement, 21,6.
3. Ibid. 36,1-2.
4. Ibid. 61,3.
5. Ibid. 64.
6. Ibid. 64.
7. Ephesians 1,1.
8. Ibid. 3,2.
9. Ibid. 7,2.
10. Ibid. 15,3; cf. 18,2; Romans 3,3.
11. Trallians 10,1.
12. Ibid. 11,1.
13. Smyrnaeans 4,2.
14. Ibid. 7,1.
15. Ibid. 8,2.
16. Ibid. 10,1.
17. Polycarp 3,2.
18. Trallians 9.
19. Polycarp 17,2-3.
20. Ibid. 19,1; 22,1.
21. Similitudes V, VI.
22. Ibid. VIII,2.
23. Ibid. XI,1.
24. Ibid. XII.
25. *The Letter to Diognetus* 8,11.
26. Ibid. 9,6.
27. Justin Martyr, *I Apology* 12,13.
28. All the writings referred to above, except Hermas's *The Shepherd*, may be found in Cyril R. Richardson, ed., *Early Christian Fathers* (New York: Macmillan, 1970). For *The Shepherd*, see Kirsopp Lake, tr., *The Apostolic Fathers*, Cambridge: Harvard University Press, 1970).

Chapter Two

1. *The Gospel of Thomas*, no. 3.
2. E. Hennecke–W. Schneemelcher (Philadelphia: Westminster, 1963).
3. *The Nag Hammadi Library* (San Francisco: Harper & Row, 1977).
4. Eusebius (cf. IV, 8, 1f.; 22, 1; II, 23, 3).

Chapter Three

1. *Against Heresies* III, 18.2.
2. Ibid. V, 21.1.
3. Ibid. V, 21.1. (The citations in this and the two preceding notes are given by William P. Loewe, "Myth and Counter-Myth: Irenaeus' Story of Salvation," in *Interpreting Tradition: The Art of Theological Reflection*, ed. Jane Kopas (Chico, Cal.: Scholars Press, 1983), pp. 49-50.
4. *Miscellanies* IV, 17 (107.55).
5. Ibid. VII, 3 (21).
6. *Exhortation* X (110).
7. *Miscellanies* VI, 9 (71).
8. Ibid. II, 25.
9. *Homily on Luke*, 29.
10. *Commentaries on Matthew*, 92 and 55.
11. *Demonstration of the Gospel* (IV, 13).
12. Ibid.
13. *On the Trinity*, 2.25.
14. *Tome*, 4.
15. *First Catechetical Instruction*, 40.
16. Sister Benedicta Ward, SLG, tr., *The Prayers and Meditations of St. Anselm* (New York: Penguin Books, 1973), p. 97.
17. Ibid. pp. 97-98.
18. Abelard, Letter 4 in *The Letters of Abelard and Heloise*, tr. Betty Radice (New York: Penguin Books, 1974), pp. 150-51.
19. Ibid. Letter 6, pp. 180-81.
20. Ibid. Letter 7, p. 185.
21. PL 195:138B.
22. Anselm, quoted in Ward, *Prayers and Meditations*, pp. 153, 155.
23. *Letter 322*, PL 182:527.
24. *Sermons 2*.
25. *De Institutione*, c. 26.

Chapter Four

1. Ch. 8. All quotations from *Legenda Maior* are from Bonaventure, *The Classics of Western Spirituality*, tr. and ed. by Ewert Cousins (New York: Paulist Press, 1978).
2. Beryl Smalley, *The Study of the Bible in the Middle Ages* (Notre Dame: University of Notre Dame Press, 1964), p. 284.
3. Ibid. p. 285.
4. *Legenda Maior*, ch. 1.
5. Ibid. ch. 2.
6. Ibid. ch. 3.
7. Ibid. ch. 3.
8. Ibid. ch. 5.
9. Ibid.
10. Ibid. ch. 3.
11. Ibid.

Chapter Five

1. *The Fire of Love*, tr. by Clifton Wolters (New York: Penguin Books, 1972), p. 92.

2. Ibid. p. 64.

3. Ibid.

4. Ibid. p. 92.

5. Ibid. p. 96.

6. Ibid. p. 98.

7. Ibid. p. 123.

8. Ibid. pp. 122, 123.

9. Ibid. p. 125.

10. Ibid. p. 129.

11. In *The Coasts of the Country*, ed. by Clare Kirchberger (Chicago: Regnery, 1952), I, pp. 151-53.

12. *The Cloud of Unknowing and Other Works*, tr. by Clifton Wolters (New York: Penguin Books, 1978), p. 89.

13. Ibid. pp. 89-90.

14. Ibid. pp. 93-94.

15. Ibid. p. 94.

16. Ibid. ch. 26-32.

17. Ibid. pp. 133-34.

18. *Julian of Norwich*, "Showings," tr. by E. Colledge and J. Walsh (New York: Paulist Press, 1978), ch. 4, the Short Text, p. 130.

19. Ibid. p. 132.

20. Ibid. p. 137.

21. Ibid. p. 138.

22. Ibid. p. 208.

23. Ibid. ch. 10, Short Text, p. 142.

24. Ibid. p. 143.

25. Ibid. p. 145.

26. Ibid. p. 216.

27. Ibid. p. 225.

28. Ibid. p. 223.

29. Ibid. p. 246.

30. Ibid. p. 259.

31. Ibid. p. 292.

32. Ibid. p. 293.

33. Ibid. p. 295.

34. Selections from the writings of the mystics mentioned above as well as others are available in *The Medieval Mystics of England*, edited and with an introduction by Eric Colledge (New York: Charles Scribner's Sons, 1961). Paper.

Chapter Six

1. John P. Dolan, ed. and trans., *The Essential Erasmus* (New York: Mentor-Omega, 1964), p. 182.

2. Ibid. p. 183.

3. Ibid. p. 185.

4. Ibid. p. 186.

5. Ibid. p. 191.

6. Ibid. p. 257.

7. Ibid. p. 74.

8. Ibid. p. 357.

9. Ibid.

10. Ibid. p. 99.
11. Saint Thomas More, *A Dialogue of Comfort Against Tribulation*, ed. Leland Miles (Bloomington: Indiana University Press, 1965), p. 208.
12. Ibid. pp. 233-34.
13. John Dillenberger, ed., *Martin Luther: Selections from His Writings* (New York: Doubleday Anchor, 1961), p. 17.
14. Ibid. p. 18.
15. Ibid. p. 17.
16. Ibid. p. 135.
17. Ibid.
18. *Tischreden* 1, 837.
19. *Tischreden* 3, 3302b.
20. John Calvin, *Institutio* II, xii, 3, 3 in the 1813 Allen translation, ed. Hugh T. Kerr, *A Compend of the Institutes of the Christian Religion* (Philadelphia: Westminster, 1939) pp. 74f.
21. *Catechismus ex Decreto Concillii Tridentini ad Parochos... Editus*, IV, 11 (Romae: Typis...de Propaganda Fide, 1945), p. 29.
22. *The Spiritual Exercises of St. Ignatius*, trans. Anthony Mottola (New York: Doubleday Image, 1964), p. 56. The selection is from a Note appended to the First Exercise of the First Week.
23. Ibid. p. 71. From "The Kingdom of Christ," Second Contemplation, Second Week.
24. Ibid. p. 82. From "The Three Modes of Humility," Second Week.
25. "Life," chap. 22, from Silverio de Santa Teresa, CD (trans.) and E. Allison Peers (ed.), *The Complete Works of Saint Teresa of Jesus*, vol. 1 (New York: Sheed & Ward, 1946), pp. 138f.
26. John Frederick Nims, *The Poems of St. John of the Cross: New English Versions*, a bilingual edition (New York: Grove Press, 1959), p. 41.

Chapter Seven

1. *A New Catechism, p. 145.*
2. *Life*, vol. 1 of *The Complete Works of Saint Teresa of Jesus*, E.A. Peers (New York: Sheed & Ward, 1946), pp. 23f.
3. Ibid. p. 54f.
4. Ibid. p. 55.
5. Ibid. p. 58; cf., "Let [the servant of God] help Him to bear the Cross and consider how He lived with it all His life long," p. 67; "I desire to suffer, Lord, because Thou didst suffer," p. 68.
6. Ibid. p. 79.
7. Ibid. p. 99.
8. Ibid. p. 136.
9. Ibid. p. 138.
10. Ibid. p. 139.
11. Ibid. p. 140f.
12. Ibid. p. 178.
13. Ibid. p. 179.
14. Ibid. p. 188.
15. Introduction to *Vejamen* (Judgment), vol. 3 of Peers, p. 216.
16. "Saint Maria Maddalena de Pazzi," in *Spear of Gold*, ed. H.A. Reinhold (London: Burns Oates, 1947), p. 269. Published in the United States by Pantheon as *The Soul Afire: Revelations of the Mystics*.
17. Jacob Boehme, *The Way to Christ*, Peter Erb (New York: Paulist, 1978), p. 93.
18. Ibid. p. 191.

19. Ibid. p. 133.

20. Saint Francis de Sales, *Introduction to the Devout Life,* and ed. John K. Ryan (New York: Doubleday Image, 1950), p. 98.

21. Ibid. p. 131.

22. Ibid. cf. p. 145.

23. Ibid. p. 168.

24. Ibid. p. 285.

25. *The Autobiography of St. Thérèse of Lisieux: The Story of a Soul,* John Beevers (New York: Doubleday Image, 1957), p. 114.

26. Ibid. p. 150.

27. Ibid. p. 151.

28. Ibid. p. 156.

Chapter Eight

1. Adolf von Harnack. *What Is Christianity?* T.B. Saunders (New York: Harper Torchbooks, 1957).

2. Wilhelm Bousset in *Theologische Rundschau* 4 (1901), 89-103, cited by Albert Schweitzer, *The Quest of the Historical Jesus,* W. Montgomery (New York): Macmillan, 1961), p. 243. The translation is from the first German edition of 1906, which was entitled *From Reimarus to Wrede: A History of Life-of-Jesus Research.*

3. Schweitzer, *Quest of the Historical Jesus* (see n. 2 above), p. 253.

4. Johannes Weiss, *Jesus' Proclamation of the Kingdom of God* (Philadelphia: Fortress, 1971). Cf. pp. 129-31. This essay of 1892 appeared in a second edition (1900) of 210 pages.

5. Rudolf Bultmann, "Introduction" to *What Is Christianity?* (see n. 1 above), p. x; written in 1950.

6. Von Harnack, *What Is Christianity?,* p. 3.

7. Ibid. pp. 73-74.

8. Ibid. p. 73.

9. Ibid. p. 77.

10. Ibid. p. 142.

11. Weiss, "Summary," *Jesus' Proclamation,* pp. 129-31.

12. Ibid. cf. p. 134.

13. Ibid. p. 136.

14. Schweitzer, *Quest of the Historical Jesus,* p. 239-41.

15. Cf. ibid. pp. 350-51.

16. Ibid., p. 402.

17. Rudolph Bultmann, *The History of the Synoptic Tradition* (New York: Harper & Row, 1963); first published as *Die Geschichte der Synoptischen Tradition,* 1921.

18. Bultmann, *Jesus and the Word* (New York: Scribner's, 1934); first published in German as *Jesus,* 1926.

19. Ibid. p. 85.

20. Günther Bornkamm, *Jesus of Nazareth* (New York: Harper & Row, 1960); German original, 1956.

21. Hans Conzelmann, *Jesus* (Philadelphia: Fortress, 1972); published as *"Jesus Christus"* in *Religion in Geschichte und Gegenwart,* 3 Aufl., III (1959), 619-53.

22. C.H. Dodd, *The Founder of Christianity* (New York: Macmillan, 1954).

23. Ibid. p. 102.

24. Ibid. p. 24.

25. Karl Adam, *Christ Our Brother*, Collier Books edition (New York: Macmillan, 1931), 1962.

26. Ibid. p. 15.

27. Ibid. p. 30.

28. Ibid. p. 33.

29. Ibid. pp. 35-36.

30. Ibid. p. 44.

31. Karl Barth, *Church Dogmatics: A Selection* IV, 1, tr. and ed. G. W. Bromiley (New York: Harper Torchbooks, 1961), pp. 118-19.

32. Ibid. III, 2, p. 168.

33. Ernst Käsemann, *Jesus Means Freedom* (Philadelphia: Fortress, 1968).

34. Edward Schillebeeckx, *Jesus: An Experiment in Christology* (New York: Crossroad, 1979).

35. Edward Schillebeeckx, *Christ: The Experience of Jesus as Lord* (New York: Crossroad, 1980).

36. "I Believe in Jesus of Nazareth; The Christ, the Son of God, the Lord," in *Consensus in Theology?* ed. Leonard Swidler (Philadelphia: Westminster, 1980), pp. 18-32. Tr. Gerard S. Sloyan.

37. Ibid. p. 23.

38. Ibid.